T0358326

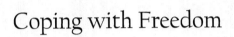

Coping with Freedom

Chantal Thomas

Coping with Freedom

Reflections on Ephemeral Happiness

Translated by Andrea L. Secara

Algora Publishing, New York
© 2001 by Algora Publishing
All rights reserved. Published 2001.
Printed in the United States of America
ISBN: 1-892941-60-0
Editors@algora.com

Originally published as *Comment supporter sa liberté*, ©
Éditions Payot et Rivages, 1998

Library of Congress Cataloging-in-Publication Data 2001—
001792

Thomas, Chantal.
 [Comment supporter sa liberté. English]
 Coping with freedom: Reflections of ephemeral happiness / by
Chantal Thomas.
    p. cm.
 ISBN 1-892941-60-0 (alk. paper)
 1. Conduct of life. 2. Liberty. I. Title.
 BJ1884 .T4613 2001
 123'.5—dc21

                                    2001—001792

New York
www.algora.com

Among the many liberties enumerated in *The Rights of Man* and so often and so complacently reiterated by the wise men of the 19th century, two rather important items have been left out: the right to contradict one's self and the right *to leave*.

Baudelaire, *L'Art romantique*

By the Same Author

Sade, L'Oeil de la lettre, Payot, 1978.

Casanova, Un voyage libertin, Denoël, "L'Infini", 1985.

Don Juan ou Pavlov. Essai sur la communication publicitaire, in collaboration with Claude Bonnange, Seuil, "La Couleur des idées", 1987, and "Points", 1991.

La Reine scélérate, Marie-Antoinette dans les pamphlets, Seuil, 1989. Published in English as *The Wicked Queen : The Origins of the Myth of Marie-Antoinette*, Zone Books, June 1999.

Thomas Bernhard, Seuil, "Les Contemporains", 1990.

Sade, Seuil, "Écrivains de toujours", 1994.

La Vie réelle des petites filles, Gallimard, "Haute Enfance", 1995.

CONTENTS

INTRODUCTION

A few years ago, in Lyon, I chose an old hotel at the edge of the Saône River as my temporary home. I liked everything about it: the wooden staircase going up to the reception desk on the first floor, the sitting room where an odd assortment of round-cornered tables and chairs communed together amid a soft, leafy tangle of potted plants, and the wreck of a library... From a seat by the window, I would watch the boats go by. Sitting there every morning, coffee cup in hand, I was suffused with a feeling of serenity and inviolability, and a groundless sense of completeness. That setting gave me a sense of being in the right place — a place that I never would have taken the trouble to go out and look for, and one that I could leave whenever I wanted to and come back without my absence having made any difference. I hadn't even bothered to explore the place. I was only familiar with a small portion of it, but enough for my purposes as an unquestioning, fleeting, intermittent visitor. Sometimes I came across other boarders, but very few; men, getting on in years, whom I thought might be musicians during a break in their touring schedule.

I felt so good sitting in the guests' lounge that I finally moved into the adjacent room: Room One. Every time I got ready to make my reservation, I would hesitate for a few seconds, then go ahead with my request; this pause was matched on the hotel's part with a moment of uncertainty while, as they said, they verified whether "my" room was free. It was. I was always glad to get there, and the man from the hotel, always pleasant and quiet, would hand me the key. However, the silhouettes of other guests became increasingly discreet and the lounge seemed emptier and emptier — in no way diminishing the harmony of this house of phantoms brought together by chance in the course of deaths and departures. But one day, perhaps to integrate myself more with the rest of the residents, to ensure myself that they still existed — or to avoid becoming a prisoner of habit — I asked for some room other than Room One, any other room.

"Don't you like it anymore?"

"Oh yes, very much (and I thought of the oval mirror above the bed, the striped curtains whose golden yellow reminded me of one of my favorite paintings, *The Harvest,* by Brueghel the Elder), but I'd like to make a change."

"I'm afraid that would be difficult. The hotel is closing. All the rooms are being renovated. Only Room One is still available to the public — and only for a short time, at that."

So, in fact, I had had no choice, for the last several months. But every time, I had been delighted to get my favorite room. . .

This story is played out in various forms all the time. Freud, Kafka, Marx and others have taught us that freedom does not exist. The very concept, according to Schopenhauer, is repugnant to human understanding. When we try to look at miracles as effects without causes, our mind is paralyzed. Freedom is just an illusion, a word that lends itself to flights of fancy, to misguided impulses, and to songs (the media constantly bombard us with "Freedom" and "Love"; we can't get away from these obsessions). This constant refrain, sung as a solo and in chorus, surrounds us so thoroughly that in the end, convinced that we are acting according to nothing but our own inclinations, we finally go along with it. Psychologically and politically, we are subjugated by forces that we are not even aware of. Our finest initiatives are only a response to the desire or to the will of others, one link in a chain of necessary events. "Even without prison, we still know that we are in prison," wrote Maurice Blanchot. How true.

The fact remains that when you really *are* in prison, it does make a difference. The law places bars between the prisoner and the world, cutting him off from his own life. His despair, whether raging or resigned, leaves him in no doubt as to how deadly his isolation is. That is why, if he tries to escape, the possibility of dying in the attempt doesn't deter him at all. "Oh, *when*, my dear friend, will my horrible situation come to an end? When, great God! will I get out of this tomb in which they have buried me alive?", exclaimed the Marquis de Sade in one of his letters from Vincennes.

Without going as far as the tragic experience of incarceration, who among us has not felt the pain, in childhood or adolescence, of finding himself cooped up behind the walls of a boarding school, a summer camp or some other place of confinement? Who hasn't choked with indignation when it is impossible to escape, or to modify, the regimentation? This is how Federico Fellini remembers the religious school run by the Salesians at Rimini, where his parents had sent him. "I remember with a feeling of deep dejection the deplorable hole of a dreadful courtyard, with its two lugubrious basketball poles and surrounded on all sides by a big wall surmounted by a metal mesh, two meters high. Beyond this fence, the little bells of the hackney carriages could be heard, the car horns, the voices, people calling to each other and walking about freely, an ice cream in their hand."[*][1]

Indeed, on the other side — the side where you

---

[*] Quotations from French sources translated by Algora Publishing.

[1]. Federico Fellini, *Faire un film*, translated from Italian into French by J.-P. Manganaro, Paris, Seuil, 1996, p. 63.

can go out without asking permission — nothing exceptional is going on. It is the fundamental banality of everyday life. But far from appeasing us, reminders of these simple gestures (sitting down on a bench, kissing a boyfriend, breathing the fresh evening air, drinking a coffee, buying the newspaper, going to the movies) are intolerable for us — precisely because they are simple and because, in the days when we could do them without thinking about it, they seemed routine, inevitable. We don't know their value until we've lost them. We think that if we could do these things again, these gestures that are so simple and so fabulous, we would do them immediately, and twice rather than once. We would just keep on cuddling our loved ones, and watch all our old-time favorites over and over again — Catherine Deneuve in *Belle de jour* (Buñuel), Humphrey Bogart in *Casablanca*, *La Notte* (Antonioni), *La Voie lactée* (Buñuel) — we'd drink champagne and margaritas, stroll or go ice-skating in Central Park, buy hyacinths and plane tickets, shop for shoes, try on hats, dream over kimonos; we would fill up our apartment with wildflowers, leave it in a big mess and use it as a cocoon to foster our metamorphoses, changing addresses the way we change shirts; we would follow our dreams; we would quit stopping ourselves from crying, or from talking with people we don't know; we would walk out of meetings and movies that are boring, jump on whatever bus comes along, even — or especially — if we don't know where it's going; read in bed, do our nails, muse over photographs by Kertész and paintings by Tiepolo, Goya, Twombly, Balthus, Mondrian, Caspar David Friedrich; amble down an endless hillside under a dusting of snow, in the full sun; eat cherries, swim in every sea and taste every wine, order immense platters of seafood and devour them under the wide gaze of Picasso's *Gobeur d'oursins* [*The Sea Urchin Eater*]. . .

Consumed by these vain desires, we are shocked by people who ignore such treasures because they have them within reach. This shock is transformed into horror when the chasm separating the "have's" from the "have-not's" is too great. Primo Levi relates the following scene from his captivity at Auschwitz, in December 1944. As a chemist, he has just been assigned to the camp factory's laboratory. And this, by sparing him from forced labor outdoors in the cold and mud, and from beatings, saves his life. In the laboratory are some German and Polish women, clean, rosy-faced girls brimming with health, who strike him as "creatures from another planet". The Jewish prisoners are dirty, stinking, famished, covered with sores, staggering from exhaustion. Of course, they have no verbal contact with these wonders from another world. But they hear them chatting among themselves.

> 'Are you going home on Sunday? I'm not, traveling is so uncomfortable!'
>
> 'I'm going home for Christmas. Only two weeks and then it will be Christmas again; it hardly seems real, this year has gone by so quickly!'
>
> .... This year has gone by so quickly. This time last year I was a free man: an outlaw, but free, I had a name and a family, I had an eager and restless mind, an agile and healthy body.... Today the only thing left of the life of those days is what one needs to suffer hunger and cold.[2]

Just a sketch of a scene, a few trivial sentences uttered in all innocence and which, in the infernal circus of cruelty, might not seem worth mentioning nor focusing on. But it is the opposite that is true.

---

2. Primo Levi, *If This is a Man*, translated from the Italian by Stuart Woolf, The Orion Press, New York: 1959; p. 168-169.

These words grip us and burn themselves into our memory forever, for the monstrous depth of unconsciousness and insensitivity from which they spring, for their very innocence. We might have said such words, ourselves; we do say them. Not in front of people who have been handed over to death camps and for whom every day is both a series of sufferings to be surmounted and the reward for their (improbable) victory the day before, but in front of regular people like us. Except that it sometimes happens that these people, too, have recently been told that they are ill, and in contrast to us (due only to a temporal shift) they, too, feel the year passing by and see it in terms of a day-to-day combat — if not in terms of seconds drawn out *ad infinitum* under the impact of pain.

The leitmotiv of *time that we do not notice passing* is a banality that we let slip, with a conventional sigh, without thinking about it. In order to have something to hold onto and not to fall straight into the black hole of lapsed memory, we counterbalance that by the notion of *time that counts.*

With considerably less emotion (since it was not the brutal separation between two worlds that was at issue, but something impossible to comprehend), I remember being shocked once, during a philosophy class — at that age when we discover that freedom is not just a theme for stormy arguments with our parents, but also a chapter to be studied in a textbook. We were reading the passage in *Phaedon* where Socrates, still in prison but released from his chains, expresses his satisfaction.

> Socrates then raising himself up in bed, bent his leg which had been fettered; and as he rubbed it with his hand, Oh my friends, he said, what a strange thing does that seem to be, which men call agreeable! . . . Had Æsop made this remark, he would probably have written the following fable: — 'The gods were willing to unite opposite sensations; but as they found it impossible, they tied them at both ends together, since which they have been constantly inseparable.' — This truth I have just experienced. These fetters gave me much pain; but they are no sooner removed than the most agreeable sensation ensues.[3]

3. Plato, *Phaedon*, translated from the German by Moses Mendelssohn. Arno Press, New York: 1973; p. 10-11.

The notion that pleasure might be only a sus-
pension of pain, that it is defined by its opposite,
both astonished me and made me sad. As if pleasure
did not have an absolute value, as if you would have
to be famished to enjoy picking raspberries, or
parched with thirst to fully taste a cool Sancerre
wine, or sick to appreciate health — to realize that it
is not just the opposite of illness, but that it implies a
sense of well-being, a certain relaxed quality, the
euphoria born from an excess of vitality! And it's the
same way with freedom — we don't experience it
only when we are deprived of it, in a prison cell, behind electrified barbed wire fences.

"I *feel* that I am free but I *know* that I am not,"
wrote Cioran. This feeling, indifferent or superior to
the knowledge that denies it, comes to us moment by
moment, in the interstices. This reflection is based
on those moments. That is to say that it is fragile, and
that it is not based on specific events that can be lo-
cated objectively, but on gaps, interruptions, lacunae.
They do not count, or so we think. They don't add up
to anything. Besides, we can't even describe them.
They are as elusive as cloudscapes seen from an air-

plane window, whose beauty overwhelms us with pleasure for a moment and which we can scarcely talk about later on. Once we have landed, our faces still bright with the azure expanse we have traversed, do we try to tell our earth-bound friends about it? About the vision of a vast vaporous plateau with monumental buildings of clouds rising out of them, buildings that miraculously held together when the plane sliced through? Or the impalpable sculpture, the glorious configuration of an inverted face of a pirate, about which I was spinning stories for my own pleasure, while sipping champagne, or the sunset that lasted for hours, imperceptibly wafting from rose to orange to mauve, to crimson, so that it seemed that the plane, whose wings reflected their nuances, also shifted to the same colors? (The only stories that seem to come out of airplane trips are accidents that were avoided, or upsetting incidents like lost luggage. As for high altitude orgasms, like in *Emmanuelle*, the principal interested parties remain discreet about their games).

Such idle moments occur even in the tightest schedules, the busiest lives. We are suddenly moved, overcome by giddiness, projected into a time before time existed, to a beach somewhere in eternity, accompanied by the strains of music. We see ourselves playing a role in a shimmering movie, and the movie is our life. Quivering, carried away by the unknown, throbbing with mystery, we turn back, disoriented, frightened, to take up our usual activities again. However, these vague, inexplicable moments, jarring as they are, may be what most makes us belong to ourselves (that pleasant sense of belonging, without any specified duration or act of ownership, that we feel in a hotel room), or at least what enables us to continue to exist. Out of curiosity. For fun.

This book was written, for the most part, while on a journey, sitting in cafés, in way-stations, in that special state of isolation and internalized concentration that paradoxically encourages attention to the surroundings, to overheard conversations and the general hubbub and background music. Perhaps because, contrary to what happens in the regimented silence of a library (where, when you take your eyes off your book, you only see more books), it is not enough to submit yourself passively to the function of a place. You have to make a subtle effort, not of opposition but of differentiation, drawing around yourself a protective screen, inside of which, observant and thoughtful, meditative and inattentive, you can settle in. It's a fantasy shelter, a kind of tent, invisible to others, which you can put up or take down in the blink of an eye. Inside this momentary studio, what come from the outside world and what comes from your books are all treated the same way — memories of a scene from your life are treated the same way as scenes from a novel or a movie. Of course, that approach causes distortions. But don't they all, since it is only when they are re-created by us and for us that people, landscapes or thoughts matter to us?

Coping with Freedom doesn't offer any practical tips or how-to's. This essay is intended, rather, as an incentive to travel, to get away. It suggests ways of living on the fringes, of recording mirages, of celebrating one's solitary state.

Marcel Proust suggests that:

> There are perhaps no days of our childhood we
> lived so fully as those we believe we left without

having lived them, those we spent with a favorite book.[4]

Let's apply that thought to our whole life, and besides reading we can add innumerable activities that, in themselves, are not justified by any practical purpose and are therefore delectable, activities that give found time its charm, the secret of having time for oneself.

---

4. Marcel Proust, *On Reading Ruskin*, translated by Jean Autret, William Burford, and Philip J. Wolfe. Yale University Press, New Haven and London: 1987; p. 99.

GOING ON STRIKE

Sometimes I come across mothers who use a leash when they take their children for a walk. They don't do it out of spite, of course; it reassures them a little; it reduces their perpetual fear of catastrophes. Besides, the child often has fun with the situation. He talks to the dog, his peer; he plays around, stops in his tracks and refuses to walk, or starts running — and immediately falls down, flailing his arms and legs. Then he cries, and screams for help. Or he may do a war dance, running around his mother and tying her up in his own restraint . . . Nonetheless, he is the one who is *bound*, and, for many years he will have no choice about his comings and goings. He can't go anywhere unless someone goes with him or unless he gives a full report. Since he is unable to provide for his own needs, since he needs support, he has no freedom but that which his parents or teachers grant to him. And that freedom has all the insipidity of what is Good. That is why children do their best to invent another one, hidden, secret, that they can recognize as their own. A clandestine freedom. This is a game that the parents are dimly aware of, without necessarily recognizing it as a form of rebellion.

As Pavese notes,

> It could be that children are more routine-minded than adults, but we do not realize it because they live at war with adults, and are forced to follow their habits in secrets. In fact, adults do their best to break all the habits of children, suspecting that they contain an element of opposition and anarchism.[1]

Pavese stresses that this war is, in an important sense, a game. For children, he says, it has the unconscious meaning of declaring independence from the adults. That is why they throw all their energies into it while the adults, for their part, try to keep things under control, constantly hollering, "Quiet down!",

---

1. Cesare Pavese, *The Burning Brand: diaries 1935-1950*, translated by A. E. Murch. Walker & Company, New York: 1962; p.159.

"Stop that!", "Simmer down!", "Pay attention!", "Chill out!", "If you keep that up, we're going home!", "Cut it out. . .", a father yells, "or I'll take away your bicycle!". "Go to the back of the car, against the wall!", a teacher orders the troop of high-schoolers she's trying to escort in the subway. . . Pavese notes that the children behave themselves for five minutes and then start over, in some new way, for the game has no limits. Playing half-heartedly is not playing at all. And not playing is boring. "It's no big deal; you can be bored for a little while without making all this fuss." And the adult might add, if he (or she) were more honest, or more lucid: "Look at us. We're bored, but we're not crying."

Fritz Zorn, in *Mars*, a diary of a disease and a testamentary autobiography, relentlessly indicts the general anesthesia of ordinary existence; with a raging heart he denounces the deadly boredom in which he was raised and educated. The boredom resounded in him through his mother's words.

> Every Sunday evening she (my mother) would call up one relative or another and tell him or her how we had spent the day. She always said the

same thing: 'We've had a nice, quiet day.' A nice, quiet day — what a horrible phrase![2]

And it's in honor of that same ideal of peace and quiet that his neighbors would scream out their windows at the children playing in the street.

> It's already quiet here, but it's got to be even quieter.... In Switzerland, peace and quiet have to reign at all times, and the demand for them is always expressed as an imperative. 'Be quiet, quiet!' people command, and the implication is 'Die, be dead!'[3]

Children are not good at being bored. That is one of the limits of their sociability, a sign of their health and vigor. Boredom drives them to tears, to tantrums. Children don't put anything into perspective, as their drawings show. Everything hits them full force, and they have no way to avoid or diminish the impact; they can't relativize. They live in the absolute, and they experience boredom in the same way. Louis XIV was worried when he saw Le Nôtre's first plans for the Menagerie at the Palace of Versailles, in

---

2. Fritz Zorn, *Mars*, translated from German by Robert and Rita Kimber. Alfred A. Knopf, New York: 1981, p. 198.
3. *Ibid*, p. 195-196.

1699; he wanted a "more childish vision throughout". Was it the designer's admirable and totalitarian perspective that disturbed him? Sometimes it is vital to forget the laws of perspective, and put oneself back into the chaos of a world where everything has equal value — and occurs instantaneously. A world where our only alternatives are to be dazzled or stricken.

Children's inability to tolerate boredom is the inverse of the absolute power that play has over them. They scream when they're bored — almost as loudly as when they're taken away from their toys. Fritz Zorn did not scream; but he did wonder whether he would survive the disease of tedium.

> I don't know if I will survive this illness. If I do die of it, it will be correct to say that death was the ultimate goal of my education.[4]

This description applies perfectly to the way Rousseau recommended educating girls, i.e. breaking them. His treatise on education is mainly about the little boy, Emile. But he does not neglect to give him a partner in schooling, Sophie.

---

4. *Ibid.*, p. 24.

Even the constraint in which she keeps her daughter, if it is well directed, will, far from weakening this attachment, only increase it; for dependence is a condition natural to women, and thus girls feel themselves made to obey. For the same reason that they have — or ought to have — little freedom, they tend to excess in the freedom that is left to them. Extreme in everything, they indulge themselves in their games with even more intensity than boys do. . . . This intensity ought to be moderated. . . . Do not allow for a single instant in their lives that they no longer know any restraint. Accustom them to being interrupted in the midst of their games and brought back to other cares without grumbling.[5]

Sophie is going to be restrained to death.

Don't answer

Children have no choice. Saying No, expressing out loud their disagreement with a plan that has been conceived for their own benefit, is impossible. They

---

5. Jean-Jacques Rousseau, *Emile or On Education*, translated by Allan Bloom. Basic Books, Inc., New York: 1979; p. 369-370.

can only subvert the "serious" activities and take maximum advantage of any permitted lapses, clinging frantically to their games. Exalted by the fire that passion ignites in us, they don't feel hungry or tired. Quiet or noisy, they're entirely absorbed, busying themselves near their parents and apparently within their sphere of control. Actually, they are not sharing the same space nor, indeed, the same time. What may be a long, pleasant afternoon for the adults goes by for the children in the flash of a trance.

They're at the beach, playing. They're building a sand castle, which the rising tide is about to destroy. Water is already pouring over the drawbridge. A tower is melting, and the building is about to collapse. The little architects struggle to repair the damage. They're not likely to succeed. It's like fighting against the day that is coming to an end. However, they persist, and by tacit agreement pretend not to hear the parents who are calling at the top of their lungs:

"Peter, Jenny, Julie, Michael!"

This is hardly the right moment — to say the least. The children run around, trying to shore up the foundations.

"All right. Here I come. You're in trouble, now."

The tone is becoming exasperated. The children don't dare play deaf anymore. They respond to the threats by begging. Ten more minutes. . . five minutes. . . one minute. . . just one, give me time to. . . . The parents promise that they'll come back tomorrow. The children jump up and down — only today counts. Out of patience and out of arguments, the parents are about to leave. They fold the beach umbrellas and start the comedy of abandonment. Okay, then! good-bye, good night! We're leaving you! And they turn their backs. Then the children's hearts start pounding. Panic looms. They abandon the waves, the friends, their masterpiece, and run toward the parents. They feel defeated but not really humiliated. The winners shouldn't feel so great for winning, they say to themselves, confusedly; but it's a feeble ploy.

The question remains, how are the parents able to resign themselves to leaving so easily? Didn't they like being at the beach? (The children will be just as shocked when they learn that vacation is over, and they're told, "It's normal, everything comes to an end" — as if that were an explanation.) They don't even try to understand. They obey and take their places in the great procession of the Return. They whine, even while playing at putting their tiny bare feet in the wide, flat footprints left by their parents.

When a child *answers back*, it's considered naughty behavior that may lead to punishment, but *not answering* is a fault that is harder to pin down. *Not answering* allows you some time, gives you a chance to get used to the idea of defeat and, especially, it adds a last few minutes to play time. While those few moments don't feel quiet right, anymore, still they provide the exaltation of postponement. That interval of feigned deafness is a kind of training in freedom not through confrontation but through avoidance, through what goes unsaid — which is even worse, in the eyes of the family, determined as it is to control everyone. Confrontation, however violent it may be, is a way of going along, of recognizing an authority.

When the child makes the discreet choice of holding back, he does not call down upon himself the wrath of the adults; but let him resolutely carry this behavior into adolescence and the age bracket prone to playing games that are less acceptable than build-

sand castles, and the family will react. Louis Aragon referred to this in his *La Défense de l'infini*, noting with his superb arrogance that,

> Contrary to common belief, it is not interest that is the principal source of family crises, but hysteria. What upsets mothers, and many fathers (for a paternal psychosis can also develop, by more mysterious ways) even more than acts of rebellion, demands for money, keeping bad company and drinking and hanging out, is that the youngster is having fun, fun that cannot be described, fun that is taking place far away and that the parents do not know about, fun that remains the property of their sons, with their blank faces: it is the personal life, from which the image of home has faded out completely.[6]

Not answering is a sign of sizing up the situation wisely. Situated somewhere between presence and absence, between giving in and rebelling, this fleeting no-man's-land has its place — like that extra stretch of beach that appears at low tide, the wet ribbon of sand that is uncovered by the ebbing flow and that will be swallowed up again by the high tide. But who, standing there waiting, can touch us, while we, shimmering in the impalpable flames of the reflections, move about

---

6. Louis Aragon, *La Défense de l'infini*, Paris, Gallimard, 1997, p. 330.

in that confusion between land and sea, in that lique-
faction of light? We know instinctively, through the
dance of our heels against the hard sand, from the
spray of salt whose bitter residue we lick on our skin:
pleasure has to be taken on our own, away from other
people.

Playing deaf has its advantages (it enables you to
avoid confrontation in a battle that is lost before it
begins), but it also has its drawbacks. Not answering
can degenerate into sulking and, beyond that, for the
apprentice rebel who does not realize how serious are
the forces being set in motion, to a muteness that can
close in on him. Children's sulks are a weapon, for
those who have so few; and more than one little boy
or girl has discovered, sooner or later, that there are
few effective countermeasures against it — observes
Michaux. And he goes on:

> Refusal. *No* to joining in, to eating, speaking,
> walking or even playing.
> The child, far more than we care to believe, is
> tempted to call a halt. . . .
> A strike, the most primitive. An adventure too, a
> world not revealed to others. . . . [7]

---

7. Henri Michaux, *Spaced, Displaced*, translated by David and Helen
Constantine. Bloodaxe Books, Newcastle upon Tyne: 1992; p. 124.

And even when we don't take the system of not responding that far, it leaves after-effects. For those who get in the habit of shamelessly retreating into silence, it lingers like a doubt. You can become so used to not answering when your name is called that you end up being attached to it only very tenuously. You can develop a fragility, a friability with relation to your social identity. It becomes difficult to answer, "present", or you might even answer to another name, any name. One day, at Orly Airport, outside of Paris, I was waiting for my flight to New York. I heard a voice over the loudspeaker announcing, "Looking for Mrs. Helen Lambert." I jumped up. The stewardess at the desk asked: "Are you Mrs. Helen Lambert?" I said No, and sat back down.

This is no big deal. Being in doubt about one's name offers rich romantic virtualities, and the absence of a sense of identity leaves you the possibility of inventing yourself. Unwillingness is a strategy that has withstood the test of time. It's economical: it requires a minimum of investment and has proven to take a terrible toll on the nerves of the adversary. It comes as no surprise to see it at the top of the list in that handbook on domestic guerrilla warfare that is

Jonathan Swift's *Directions to Servants*, wherein he as-
serts:

> When your master or lady calls a servant by
> name, if that servant be not in the way, none of you
> are to answer, for then there will be no end of our
> drudgery: and masters themselves allow, that if a
> servant comes when he is called, it is sufficient.[8]

And if you think the master might be calling for you,
how should you respond? Should you rush to answer?
Not at all:

> Never come till you have been called three or
> four times; for none but dogs will come at the first
> whistle; and when the master calls 'Who's there?'
> no servant is bound to come; for 'Who's there' is
> nobody's name.[9]

And the same holds true if, indeed, it is you they are
calling. Keep quiet, no need to be over-zealous.

> If your master calls you by name, and you hap-
> pen to answer at the fourth call, you need not
> hurry yourself; and if you be chidden for staying,
> you may lawfully say you came no sooner because
> you did not know what you were called for.[10]

---

8. Jonathan Swift, *Directions to Servants*. The Golden Cockerel Press,
Waltham Saint Lawrence, Berkshire: 1925; p. 1.
9. *Ibid*, p. 2.
10. *Ibid*, p. 4.

In this hilarious, caustic text, which usually brings a smile even on the gloomiest day, Swift proposes many other battle techniques — for example, how to never take the blame when the master is yelling at you, but rather to pass it off on the dog, the cat, a monkey, a parrot, a child, or a servant who was recently let go. Or, indeed, how to justify an unjustifiable delay by inventing a thousand excuses along these lines:

> Your father sent you to sell a cow, and you could not get a chapman till nine at night; you were taking leave of a dear cousin who is to be hanged next Saturday.
>
> . . . . Some nastiness was thrown on you out of a garret window, and you were ashamed to come home before you were cleaned, and the smell went off.
>
> . . . . You were told your master had gone to a tavern, and came to some mischance, and your grief was so great, that you inquired for his honour in a hundred taverns between Pall Mall and Temple Bar.[11]

From the pleasure of telling stories to the joy of

---

11. *Ibid.*, pp. 1-2. Along the same lines, remember Truffaut's movie, *Les 400 Coups*, in which the child gives the excuse: "My mother died," to justify his absence from school.

doing all kinds of stupid things (one of nicest is the suggestion that, when the candlestick is broken, you should place the candle in a marrowbone or an old shoe or stick it to the wall with a piece of butter), Swift covers a range of actions specifically intended for servants, but which apply to children as well, since both are groups that cannot speak up for themselves. Seen through Swift's eyes, such gestures of sabotage and of laziness, inept and disastrous initiatives, the destructive genius of servants make us think of the Marx Brothers or of the universe of *Zéro de conduite*, by Jean Vigo. They all offer ways to undermine the society of the grand, from the bottom — by never missing a chance to make fun of it.

Nobody wants to take the place of the parents, the Masters, the people in power. Everything should stay the way it is. It was lousy from the start. We just muddle along, with makeshift solutions and limited interventions, modestly doing our best to make it worse. And that really makes us laugh.

Taking the viewpoint of the caste of the invisible, Swift was describing the collapse of the *Ancien Régime*. It was manifestly clear that, with this kind of service and incapable of doing anything on its own, the nobility would not get far. Two centuries later, having watched (and participated in) the collapse of the bourgeois lifestyle, Guy Debord makes this reflection in his short *Panégyrique* (a superlative example of the rhetoric of non-consent). "I have never seen a bourgeois man doing any work, given the lowness that their special kind of labor inevitably comprises; and perhaps for that reason I was able to learn, from this indifference, something good about life — albeit only by what was wrong or was missing."[12]

"Just one more moment, Mister Executioner!"

The last favorite of King Louis XV, the Countess du Barry, born Jeanne Bécu, was a true pleasure professional. Her face was so sweet that, in her youth, she was nicknamed "Lange" (L'Ange, "The Angel"). Long before she made her way to Versailles, a police report mentions her in this context: "All our pleasure-seeking high-rollers flock around her." By the time of the Revolution, Mme. du Barry was fifty years old. Wealthy, still beautiful, she seemed to be the very incarnation of the degeneration of morals during

---

12. Guy Debord, *Panégyrique*, T 1, Paris, Gallimard, 1993, p. 25.

the *Ancien Régime*, of the corruption and libertine conduct among the aristocracy, and the weakness of the kings. The Revolutionaries went after her in the château of Louveciennes, where she had been exiled by order of Louis XVI, and in December 1793 she was brought before the Revolutionary Tribunal. Fouquier-Tinville demanded the death sentence for this "infamous conspirator". He concluded his indictment with this peroration: "Yes, Frenchmen, we swear: the traitors will perish and freedom alone will remain. It has withstood and it will continue to withstand all the efforts of the despots united against us, of their slaves, their priests, and their infamous courtesans. The people, with this horde of brigands in league against it, will bring down all its enemies."

Imminent death did not elicit any heroic gestures from Mme. du Barry while she was being hauled to the scaffold. Riding on the cart, she moaned, struggled, and screamed that it was all a mistake. Instead of projecting herself into an image of something greater than herself — which those who preceded her (Charlotte Corday, Marie-Antoinette, Mme. Roland) had done so well — she shook with terror, dissolved in tears, collapsed in weakness. She was completely undignified and gave a brilliant demonstration that an existence devoted to pleasure is not the best preparation for death. Mme. du Barry had devoted herself to refining other talents: she knew how to enjoy and how to make others enjoy. She loved perfumes, ribbons, jewels, the look in men's eyes, their sex, their hands. And on that delicious background of quivering, caresses, and orgasms, just as she was to be tossed under the blade of the guillotine, she burst forth with this plea: "Just one more moment, Mister Executioner!" Among all the famous last words that the French Revolution inspired in its victims, so many of which (whether authentic or invented) have enough strength and haughty pride to serve as inscriptions on monuments to the dead, this pitiful prayer is striking.

Mme. du Barry's plea to be allowed to live for just a moment longer is stunning. She reminds us that in addition to universal principles and the Utopia of political abstractions, there is one criterion by which we evaluate our existence (subjective no doubt, and fanatical in its own way), and that is the consideration of nothing but the pleasure that it gives us. This intimate measure of delight hardly encour-

ages the collective mentality, the sense of social responsibility. It does not incline us to make sacrifices,
it turns us away from the flames of glory and deprives
death of any grandeur (the witnesses noted "the
dreadful wail" of the condemned, at the sight of the
blade). It gives us only one desire: to go on as we are.
Why? Because we like it. And even if old age re-
stricts our range and limits the array of pleasures we
can enjoy, enough remains to keep us from readily
offering ourselves up to the Executioner.

The education of Chateaubriand

It's the desire to remain forever on the shore that
so enchants us: Chateaubriand, expressing the wish
to be buried on the Grand-Bé peninsula that connects
St. Malo to the mainland at low tide, expressed this
desire literally. He asked that his tomb be placed
where he had taken his first steps.

> It is there, on the seashore between the Château
> and Fort Royal, that the children gathered to-
> gether; it is there that I was brought up, a compan-
> ion of the waves and the winds. One of the first
> pleasures I ever tasted was battling with the
> storms, and playing with the waves which re-

treated before me or chased after me on the shore.[13]

He wasn't using the waves as toys, but as playmates. He would run away or run ahead of them, and it's not clear who was leading the game. It was a fusional alliance, it was immersion in a rhythm, the art of singing with the sirens, allowing oneself be drawn into the depth of the abysses without actually shipwrecking. During his life of wandering, Chateaubriand could not keep away from the sea.

"This took place in 1788. I had horses, and I would travel through the countryside, or I would gallop through the waves, my groaning former friends; I would jump down from the saddle and play with my horse." He often lived in rooms like the room in which he was born, whose windows looked out on "a sea that extends as far as the eye can see."

Chateaubriand's lullabies were "the unisonance of the waves." His style was modeled on the horizon of a seascape. Reading his phrases is like scanning the surf, and it is the sound of the sea that animates his rhetoric. Perhaps Chateaubriand also owes to the sea

---

13. François-René de Chateaubriand, *The Memoirs of Chateaubriand*, translated by Robert Baldick. Alfred A. Knopf, New York: 1962; p. 18-19.

his love of freedom, in the spirit of Baudelaire's famous poem, *Man and the Sea* ("Free man, you will always cherish the sea!/The sea is your mirror; you contemplate your soul/In its infinitely unfolding sur-
face...").

Certainly he does, to some extent; but he also
ascribes his sense of liberty, decisively, to his aristo-
cratic origins:

> I was born a gentleman. In my opinion, I have
> profited by this accident of the cradle, keeping
> that steadfast love of liberty which is the special
> characteristic of an aristocracy whose last hour
> has struck."[14]

Chateaubriand derived from his birth (and from his
father's example) a radical sense of insubordination.
"I have in me something that makes obeying an impossibility", he declared, with irrefutable tranquility.
This "impossibility" was reinforced by his spending
time, playfully as well as contemplatively, with the
sea. He owes his disposition as a dreamer to the sea,
to its relentlessly shifting currents; and that magic
portal that always allows him to withdraw from the

---

14. *Ibid.*, p. 4.

torment of an obligatory activity and turn inward to his internal theater — to dream with his eyes open, leaving an illusory marionette on display to onlookers. At Brest, where he was sent as a very young man to complete his education as a "guard in the navy", he ignored his schoolmates, and turned inward in his loneliness.

> The sea which I was to meet with on so many coasts washed, at Brest, the tip of the Armorican Peninsula: beyond that prominent cape there lay nothing but a boundless ocean and unknown worlds; my imagination revelled in this infinity."[15]

I have evoked the image of the seashore because I myself am still attached to it. Indeed, it embodies the miracle of circularity. "On the beach we spend time and that time never relates to anything but the beach,"[16] wrote Marc Augé. The beach is where I came to my solidest certainties, the ones on which I continue to base my life — despite their being anchored in soft, shifting ground upon which, by definition, nothing durable is built. I lived at the beach, as

15. *Ibid.*, p. 51.
16. Marc Augé, *L'Impossible Voyage, Le tourisme et ses images*, Paris, Payot & Rivages, Petite Bibliothèque, 1997, p. 49.

a child. Of course, that is over, now. The beach is no longer my principal home. But what has not ended is the revelation of how important each moment is, in whose fiery features the course of those summer days was emblazoned — whole seasons where nothing happened. Seasons where, from the outside, every day seemed to resemble the day before (without this apparent monotony diminishing their fascination). What has not changed is the absolute priority granted only to what mattered to me. I knew that that was negligible by comparison to the so-called real world. I had no illusion as to the importance of my games in the eyes of other people. But this lack of proportion did not lessen my passion in the least. It left it unscathed, measurable only by my own internal scale. That is an order of measurement that is profoundly different from the ones used by Society and History and, in a certain sense, from the Human scale. The child who grows up at the seaside feels as close to the fish and the crabs as to his "peers". And when they try, at school, to inculcate in him the concept of fundamental differences, he will always have his doubts... He will live with the awareness of being a little bit different, in terms of space, the senses, the imagination — and time, too: he knows how to read the tides, so why should he learn how to read the clock?

The beach is the ideal place for coming to that self-knowledge, that force of distance and independence, that ease that comes to us from all the time spent "playing". It is the perfect place for learning — without a teacher. Photographer Jacques-Henri Lartigue, whose talent is so closely linked to the spirit of childhood, says, "The beach is the most immense place on Earth. You can run there 'unfettered', and nobody yells at you to pay attention."[17] And the beach is not the only place. Any place can serve as an ideal terrain (the mountains, the countryside, a barn, a garden, a stretch of sidewalk, a corner of the room), if growing up there can equip us with a sense of imagination and a sense of autonomy. If, without being monitored, and to our heart's desire, we can run around there, unfettered, without anybody yelling at us to pay attention.

---

17. J.-H. Lartigue, *Mémoires sans mémoire*, Paris, Robert Laffont, 1975, p. 19.

JUST PASSING THROUGH

Pure desolation: the solitary woman, according to Michelet

Jules Michelet, who was intoxicated differently but just as surely by the blood spilled by the Revolution and by the menstrual flows of his young wife Athénaïs, noted in his journal (on September 26, 1868) that since 1857 he had written *Love, Woman, Insects, The Sea, The Mountain, The Bible of Humanity*, and the entire ending of *History of France* in the same spirit — a spirit of empathic intelligence and compassion — especially with regard to woman. ("She is everywhere", he writes of the sea. "She is a somewhat violent mother, but in the end, a mother".) He presents her to us as a weak being, a creature made to suffer, with questionable chances of survival if she follows her vocation and no chance at all if she strays from it.

One can only imagine a woman being, if not happy (that would imply a vitality that she, by nature, does not have), at least in harmony with her destiny, so long as she is married and a mother — although maternity is, alas! so often mortal. Woman is an inexhaustible subject of affliction. Think of woman, and tears come to your eyes. Trying to define her is tantamount to founding a religion, it is like probing a wound. Michelet, who had the thirst of a vampire, could not tear himself away. This description holds for the "normal" woman, that is, one who is the partner of a man. And the picture seems black enough. However, it is only a pale gray compared to Michelet's vision of the woman alone. Women are weak, and are soon destroyed by physical labor. Moreover, they are unable to maintain a sustained intellectual effort. Studying makes them sick. And when they apply themselves to it, in spite of all, it is only out of masochism:

> I have sometimes, in an omnibus, met a young
> girl, modestly attired, always wearing a hat, whose
> eyes were fixed on a book, and never once raised.
> Seated close to her, I have observed it without

staring. Most frequently, the book was some gram-
mar, or one of those manuals of examination. Little
books, thick and compact, in which all the sci-
ences are concentrated in a dry, undigested form,
as if they were flint. Nevertheless, she put it all
into her stomach, that young victim.[1]

As for passing the examinations that are essential to a career, that is likely to be enough to kill her.

To each, also, should be left the choice of the day
for her examination. To many, the trial is terrible,
and without this precaution might endanger their
lives.[2]

Woman cannot be materially self-sufficient. She is
obviously dependent. The concept of a woman's job
is a contradiction in terms.

While this description of the situation was true
enough in Michelet's day, the historian did not discuss it in the context of social circumstances but as a
final and immutable condition. Actually, according
to Michelet, a woman cannot be self-sufficient either
materially or psychologically. Her inability to earn a
living, to play an active role in society, is the expres-

---

1. Jules Michelet, *Woman*, translated from the French, last Paris edition,
by J. W. Palmer. Rudd & Carleton, New York: 1860; p. 35.
2. *Ibid.*, p. 36.

sion of a far greater handicap: a deficit in being, which results in her needing a man in order to blossom, to become herself fully. The woman without a man ends up begging, or living immorally. Rejected from the warmth of a home, she is abandoned to that horror: *living alone.*

With all his hallucinatory verve, Michelet paints a nightmarish scene: a woman alone in a room. She lives frugally, on meager wages. Every day of the week is a sinister repetition. Her days off are dreadful. And on those days, while she is just killing time, morose, she hears the sounds of partying coming from the apartments inhabited by men. The single men like to get together to celebrate their freedom, while the poor girl, stuck behind her door, is sick with fear and shame. Because, fundamentally, she feels that by moving into a furnished room on her own, however proper she may be, she has crossed the boundary that propriety sets for people of her gender. The men stuff themselves, tell racy stories, sing off-tune and all evening persecute their solitary neighbor with their raucous laughter. And sometimes they go farther.

She avoids making a noise, because a curious neighbor — some stupid student, or young clerk, perhaps — might apply his eye to the key hole, or abruptly enter to offer his services.[3]

Her room is a prison. Where can she go? To a café, a bar, a restaurant?

> What obstacles present themselves to the solitary woman! She can scarcely go out in the evening; she would be taken for a 'girl'. There are a thousand places where only men are seen, and if anything should bring her there, they are surprised, and laugh sillily.
>
> For example, suppose she is belated on the skirts of Paris, and hungry, she dare not enter a restaurant she would cause a sensation, make herself a sight; every eye would be fixed upon her, and she would hear reckless and unpleasant conjonctures.[4]

Michelet's message is clear: the bachelor leads a merry life (a boy's life, which he buries with great fanfare the day before he gets married — and get married, he must — Michelet doesn't joke around with those egoists who refuse to marry). But the single woman withers away. Her life is just a long drawn-

---

3. *Ibid.,* p. 33. And this avid helpfulness is still with us. Traveling in Mexico, I was awakened one day at 4:00AM by the night watchman, who was concerned that I might need help figuring out how to work the lavatory!

4. *Ibid,* p. 33.

out agony. Being alone is a curse, a burden. "An un-married woman can be recognized at first glance", says Michelet.

The single woman's fate is deplorable, but that of an educated woman or a woman who writes is practically inexpressible. By tradition, men have a phobia of women who write. Between the sniggers of superiority, false pity and frank hostility, women writers don't get much sympathy from men. The reverse, of course, cannot be said. Women have al-ways been ready to love male writers. As partners, hostesses, friends or Muses, they have always en-couraged their work, hosting salons and receptions where they can enjoy shelter and approval, organiz-ing readings of their works, relaxing them with pleasant conversation (intelligent women do not show any trace of that pedantry that we are taught is characteristic of the learned woman or bluestock-ing, an object of ridicule). In a short work entitled *On Women*, Diderot emphasizes "the advantages, for a man of letters, of spending time with women". Men are flattered by their company, and women can also be of material assistance, and lend them the model for those great female figures about which they can go on expounding.

In Michelet's view, one might feel just as sorry as possible for the solitary woman; but if she should dare to take pride in her state and claim to be heroic, then the phenomenon is beyond all understanding. Meditating on the portrait of Charlotte Corday, whose head, according to a contemporary journalist, "was a fury of readings of all kinds", Michelet said he initially was tempted to love her:

> The painter has created in man an eternal regret.
> No one can see her without saying within himself:
> 'O, why I was born so late! O, how much I would
> have loved her!'[5]

But then he takes it back: he has recognized in her "the demon of loneliness".

Michelet published *Woman* in 1859, and in it he shows that he had the demon of exaggeration — a demon that came to him shortly after writing *Witchcraft, Sorcery and Superstition* in 1862, a work in which he recognizes and exorcizes the qualities that living alone gives to a woman. He pushes them to the extreme and brings them all to life in that magical being, that lucid-enlightened, satanic, sibylline figure

5. Jules Michelet, *The Women of the French Revolution*, Henry Carey Baird, Philadelphia: 1855; p. 231-232.

who may harm or heal, who is at the same time an evil-doer and a victim. . . the Witch:

> Where is her lurking-place? In untracked wilds, in impenetrable forests of bramble, on blasted heaths, where entangled thistles suffer no foot to pass. She must be sought by night, cowering beneath some old-world dolmen. If you find her, she is isolated still by the common horror of the countryside; she has, as it were, a ring of fire round her haunts.[6]

Michelet breaks the circle and restores the voice that he had forbidden us from hearing. Thus he gives room for a woman's destiny in history. Mediator of "feminine electricity", he transports himself in the trances of the Sabbath. But he still does not come close to understanding that chilling scene: a woman dancing alone in her room.

One may wonder whether this concept of incompleteness, of waiting, associated with the image of a woman alone in her room, is not shared or at least tacitly accepted more broadly than one might think. By men, who cannot see a woman on the terrace of a café without thinking that she came there in the hope

6. Jules Michelet, *Witchcraft, Sorcery, and Superstition*, previously published as *Satanism and Witchcraft*. Carol Publishing Group Edition, New York: 1995; Introduction, p. 15.

of meeting someone. And maybe also by women, those who went straight from their parents' supervision to marriage, and thus never knew that short and recurring sigh of relief that comes from feeling you are at home, away from any threat of intrusion. But also, perhaps, by those women who have lived alone, for a longer or shorter period, not in sorrow and frustration but in euphoria — probably because those are times that don't make for good anecdotes — there are no witnesses, they are hard to weave into any story and so do not come up in conversation; like the cloudscape seen from the airplane, they fade away from one's memory, they are invisible or are tinged with a hint of unreality. There are whole periods of our existence, months or years, sometimes the most decisive ones, that fall into the category of the improbable. Since we do not consciously make reference to them while we are living them, they are deprived of solidity. We do not have words to remember them by. It is as if those times never existed, it seems to us. Perhaps, indeed, they never took place. . . So we give up, and allow our view of those times to slide toward the stereotypes, the images imposed from without. The scenes start to take on the

half-light of melancholy, or the white glare of schizo-
phrenia like Edward Hopper's paintings. The fact of
living alone, especially for a woman, represents something indefensible, unacceptable, both in the language and the social representation; something deval-
ues it in the eyes of the world, so that women are unable to claim it as a sign of strength, as a life skill that
they have developed.

In a maid's room

And yet if I stop to think what was the essential
revelation of my life as a student, I owe it to the dazzling new way of living. I acquired my own address, I
had a place of my *own*. If anyone asked whether I
lived with my parents, I could answer, "No, I have my
own place."

My place. I was so pleased. Not at the moment
when the landlady was showing me the room, but
when I went back on my own, to move in; having suc-
ceeded in opening the door, I paused on the threshold
of my few square feet of living space to contemplate
the still empty expanse of the hours and the days to
come. I had a joyful presentiment. I sensed that I had

been altered by the powers of this new home: and in a way, more abstractly, I felt quicker and lighter in spirit, with a pure sense of being, without the burden of attitudes projected from the outside nor any restraints imposed by the will of others. In my room, again, I had all the time in the world. It was that pleasure of having uninterrupted time. The rediscovered taste of time for play. That is why the room did not beckon me to enter: I could stand on the threshold indefinitely (like that character in Kafka's novella, or short story, *The Burrow*, who finds his place so wonderful that he never goes inside but stays in the entryway forever, in admiration). It didn't matter at all. According to how time was reckoned in that room, there was nothing in relation to which I could be behind schedule, and, in relation to its space, there was no place that I was supposed to come and fill. What satisfaction I felt when I closed the door behind me and shoved my bag up against the bed. In this alien Paris, which I was quite unfamiliar with at the time, my first room (like the soft rectangle of a towel spread out on the beach) offered me the secure contours of a shelter.

It was tiny, narrow and long (a very short

"long") and had a round window looking out at the sky. The room had one piece of furniture: an old armoire (a period piece, as Odette would have said in *Swann in Love*), in which my landlady, the Marchioness of X, had had her housekeeper leave a basin so that I could get water from the common tap on the sixth floor. I was touched by the attention. My new situation was an immediate joy for me — just as I had been struck immediately by how unhappy dormitory living would make me. When I went to boarding school, I instantly understood how miserable the nights were going to be for me. Unhappiness oozed from the staircase, dripping with "Knowledge"; we all climbed up it in single file, girded in shapeless smocks that, when I saw my reflection in a mirror, made me look like those chairs in a widow's house, all smothered in dustcovers. Unhappiness was even more perceptible in the first hall, at the end of which was the Supervisor's room (I did not envy her — her fate seemed even worse than ours. Privately, I called her *the prisoners' prisoner*; and I called her *the quintessential bitch* when I heard her, in the darkness before dawn, echoing the noise of the alarm clock, tapping the foot of my bed to get me up).

Finally, this dreadful unhappiness burst into utter misery when I came to the last room, which also abutted a supervisor's room, next to which were the washrooms and showers, and where an identical narrow, high, metal bed waited for me, dominating an identical, minimal bit of space — the bed on which I was supposed to climb up and go to pieces, exhausted. This apparatus extinguished any remaining spark of joy. The goal was reduced to merely holding out: to avoid smashing my head against the mirror, not to strangle in her sleep the one whose bunk was under mine. I couldn't stand the noise of her breathing. I knew it immediately: this perch would never become mine. For what is a bed that I only had the right to occupy at certain hours, and only for sleeping? A bed that I could never meet again in daylight, rumpling it in the afternoon, overlaid as it would be with luminous spots that would cover us together, bathe us in the same hues, the tumble of bedcovers and our naked skins — making us, to some extent, one. It was against the rules to go into the dormitory during the daytime. That struck me as being exactly like the rules in jail that force the prisoner to spend day and night in his cell. He can stay in bed all day.

But that does not make it his. Like the bars on his window or the slot through which he is monitored, that bed of frustration is just one more part of the torment he suffers.

Unless the lack inverts itself and becomes a sufficiency, and one's own caresses give birth to the most beautiful loving. Genet writes,

> [The] pleasure of the solitary, [the] gesture of solitude that makes you sufficient unto yourself, possessing intimately others who serve your pleasure without their suspecting it, a pleasure that gives to your most casual gestures, even when you are up and about, that air of supreme indifference toward everyone and also certain awkward manner that, if you have gone to bed with a boy, makes you feel as if you have bumped your head against a granite slab.[7]

I liked my first room, on the rue Notre-Dame-des-Champs, from the moment I first saw it. That does not mean that I immediately appreciated all the splendors it held. For they were not on display, for ready contemplation, but had to be discovered in the course of living there. They existed within those

7. Jean Genet, *Our Lady of the Flowers*, translated by Bernard Frechtman. Grove Press, New York: 1963; p.139.

ephemeral moments that combine to make up a field of leisure. There was, for example, the way the room looked when I was half-awake, when a dim light (which never really brightened, as is so often the case in Paris, but was content merely to serve as an indica-tion that the night was over) would seep through the diamond-paned curtains, modeling the carved trim of the armoire and exaggerating its size in the remnants of my dreams, to which I would quickly return. There was the way the room felt on rainy days. It would become one with the reading space that I had submerged myself in, it vibrated at the same fre-quency, it was suspended on the same impatience. Only hunger could pull me out of there. On rainy days, splendidly gray days — days folded to the size of the page, caught in the snare of the room's invisible depths, its impalpable internalizing force. . . I had crossed continents, and centuries; or kept wandering around in circles; and suddenly, it was evening. I would turn on a light without taking my eyes off my book. My life was evaluated in terms of the book; everything was evaluated in terms of the book. And the room, hypnotized like my body, fell under the Book's spell. Not only did it avoid creating any obstacle or distraction to my reading, but I felt it snuggling closer to me (if that were possible in a space so tight that, if I stretched out my arms, I could touch both walls!), the better to protect me, to isolate me. And then there was the satisfaction of going up to my room, breaking away from the official habitat, turning my back, at the entryway, on the name list by the concierge's desk and breathlessly climbing up the back staircase to my hideout, incognito.

Staying out late

I liked going home. I would take my time, to make the pleasure last longer. I would stop at the corner of the rue de Rennes and Notre-Dame-des-Champs to drink a beer. Usually, a fleet of tired men would be moored at the bar, and I would recognize the laugh of one of the regulars: an architect who found it only too true, as the old proverb says, that "liquor kills — but very slowly"; he didn't have the nerve to accelerate the process. That man, whom I saw almost every evening for a year, once told me, "You have the eyes of a spy." Had he guessed that I had figured him out? He finally threw himself out the window from the tenth floor of a building that he had designed.

He used to tell a great story about a skyscraper whose windowpanes had been cut a just a shade too small, so that they were not quite secure in their frames. One day when the wind came up strong, they all blew out at the same time. I particularly liked that anecdote. I could just imagine the panic of the people caught in that cataclysm of shattered glass, and their fear of being killed by these things gone wild. The narrator's laughter would ratchet up a few notches. If he had the energy to go on, he would remark: the panes fell because they were so discouraged by all the faces they were supposed to contemplate without even wincing. And he would look at us so intently, the way an actor does, on stage, in the passages of the text where the author addresses himself directly to public. I would order another beer. Once the laughter got very loud, and lasted too long. He went on laughing until he was verging on hysteria; the sound began to set off sinister waves among the audience. Perhaps as a way to escape, a man turned toward me and asked, "Are you free this evening?" I said "Yes — but please allow me to remain so."

I had to be specific, for when I only say "Yes, I am free," the interlocutor translates that into his own language and it usually comes out as, roughly: "OK, take me, give me something to do, distract me. Relieve me of my availability, my weightlessness. Before my lips even touch the fresh foam of this beer, let me dispossess me of myself and place myself in your hands, at least until tomorrow." When a man asks a woman, "Are you free?" (or "are you alone?", which everyone seems to think is the same thing — and, judging from how often that question is asked, apparently not everyone sees it with the jaundiced eye of Michelet!) he means it in the same way that a person inquires, at the movies or in a train, "Is this seat available?" Yes. OK, then he'll take it. There is no reason for it to remain free. It is a useless vacuum. The comparison may appear shocking; it is constant. It is inconceivable that a woman would take pleasure in having a drink, alone, at night in a bar, or walking along a beach or wandering through the winding streets of a foreign city. She is not free, in the sense that that term implies a positive force, a spirit that, opposed, could become heroic and incite admiration. She is disoriented. She is lost, unhinged, or is wandering randomly because she is missing something.

And what might that be? It has always and everywhere been described the same way. Michelet pointed it out to us, and by now it is only the echo of something obvious: she lacks a man's love. In *The Unbearable Lightness of Being*, Kundera writes, "But in the love poetry of every age, the woman longs to be weighed down by the man's body."[8] Men who approach women in public places are speaking as poets, sharing that faith in the female eagerness to be ballasted with the weight of a man, in chronic need of loving, which supposedly keeps us from ever having direct access to the ability to just enjoy being. When a man asks a woman, in the bar I mentioned or any of the innumerable other bars in the world, on a memorable or a forgettable night, "Are you free?" he does not stop to think that she may be enjoying this moment of availability, or even that she may have just left a lover, and is savoring the softness of the remaining night, still young.

What? She might have left her lover, after making love? Just like that, and then gone to have a

---

8. Milan Kundera, *The Unbearable Lightness of Being*, translated from the Czech by Michael Henry Heim. Harper & Row Publishers, New York: 1984; p. 5.

drink? "After making love he had an uncontrollable craving to be himself,"[9] Kundera wrote about his character. A man. But the same could be true of a woman. But for her to feel that desire, much less express it, would require her to break with tradition, to fly in the face of all those romantic, ancestral images of the happy couple, so rigid and stereotyped that the very thought of straying, even slightly, is enough to make her paralyzed. But what she is experiencing has never been described — much less represented a thousand times in all the pictorial, cinematographic, photographic traditions. Especially in photographs: it is always a couple, smiling, dressed up, arms around each other, engaged; or surrounded by the ethereal whiteness of lilies and fragrances, at their wedding, and soon thereafter with babies in their arms. And a change of surroundings is always required — a change of ideas: the couple goes on vacation, they travel, they "do" Istanbul, Venice, Greece, Australia, Tahiti, Cuba, Bruges, South Africa, Corsica, Vietnam, the Sahara. . . They are always together. The same mirror-image smiles, eyes blinded by the sun.

When it is the man who experiences this

---

9. *Ibid.*, pp. 14-15.

"uncontrollable" desire to be alone, after the love-making, he has trouble imposing that on his partner. But what happens if it is *she* who, gently disengaging, retrieves her panties from the foot of the bed and then, hair unbrushed and blouse buttoned crookedly, tries to slip out? Then this desire to be by one's self is even harder to explain. Ideally, the lover will have fallen asleep at once. Otherwise, she's going to have to do a lot of talking, affirming and repeating that it was fine, that she's happy, that she loves him, that it's because it was so good that she wants to be alone; nothing will do — he will be convinced of the opposite. He will be certain that if she leaves, it's because she is unhappy, dissatisfied, or in love with another man and is going back to him. No, no, I only love you. . . Any attempts to explain will only accentuate the misunderstanding. Finally, she may give up and resign herself to staying. And let us pray, on behalf of them both, that this does not open the gates to that hell of mutual insomnia, to be suffered side by side, mute, eyes open in the pitch dark, trying to breathe quietly, in the sweat of heat and anguish. Time stops, and the distance between them grows. They're so far apart now that she can't leave anymore. She can't even roll over or sigh out loud. The oppressive scene of the tragedy closes in on her. The bed that just so recently was as light as a hot air balloon now prefigures the double tomb of marriage, under the gravestone.

She can also refuse to give in, and leave anyway. But she won't go with the same spring in her step. And the night, for her, will have lost its charm and limpidity — its silence. Because she'll be entering it with her mind in a turmoil, continuing the argument in her head, looking for other excuses, other arguments, other reasons to offer. She is a woman inhabited by the chaos of the conflict, or a woman obsessed — a woman who now, in any situation, alone or with her friends, male or female, will still be talking to that person whom she failed to convince, to mold according to her liking. How many times do we overhear conversations in a restaurant, at lunch-time, between two women who only talk "to each other" in order to harp on how badly they were treated in a divorce, how hurt they have been by a betrayal, citing all the evidence of selfishness and lack of understanding, of ingratitude — always from her viewpoint, blaming Him, the Traitor. Or Them, the children; they have their own life to live, of course, but still. . .

Lunch-time was a break during which they could have had some fun. That is precluded by the fatal cross they bear, their obsession. They are in a hurry to do just one thing, they have only one thirst; before they even get around to ordering a bottle of mineral water, they turn to the topic that tortures them, to the resentment that eats away at them. In their parallel monologues, in the sentences that they have repeated so often, you can hear the echo of bloody scenes — the noise level can be sensed. Because, in such scenes, the noise level is reassuring; they talk loudly in the vain hope that this external, noisy event, real and present as it is, will take the place of that other, internal, quiet, and irrevocable event — the break-up — and spare them the pain. However, it is inevitable that at a certain point *the noise stops*. What we learn during years of living alone is silence. And if I make a game of prolonging the last rites of going home, if I spend time hanging out at the bar, it is for the pleasure of drinking and of listening to the conversations there. Alcoholics are free, compared to the rest of the world, the way the jester is compared to the king. They have the right to say anything, because it doesn't matter. There may be flashes

of genius in what they say, but they too are of no consequence. By morning, it will all be gone. The flashes
of awareness that may emanate from all this waste,
from this hodge-podge of the finest resources of an
intelligence, arouse tones of radical pride in the
drunk — at the very moment when he is rolling lower
than the dirt. He despises, in one fell swoop, the slav-
ing masses of working serfs, the bowing and scraping
club of courtiers, and the king himself. Guy Debord
artfully describes this sense of sovereignty:

> At first I liked, as everyone does, the feeling of
> slight intoxication; then very soon I liked what is
> beyond violent intoxication, when the line has
> been crossed: a splendid and terrible peace, the
> true taste of the passage of time.[10]

This habit of staying out as long as possible
amid the hubbub of the cafés also had to do with the
art (some kind of inverted musical art, I suppose) of
heightening my perception of the moment when I
would turn my back on this noisy realm where, in the
night-time calm of the building's courtyard, I would
anticipate the silence of my room. At the foot of the
staircase, a little enamel plaque pointed with an au-

---

10. Guy Debord, *Panégyrique, op. cit.,* p. 43.

thoritative finger to the service entrance. This was a leftover from the 19th century (like the faded signs on certain façades where you can barely make out: "Gas on all floors"), a vestige of an era when the servants, essential wheels in the strictly stratified machinery of bourgeois society, belonged to a class that did not mingle with the Masters. "When your work is done, go back to your hole and don't let us see you moping about in our areas", said the finger with the manicured nail. To me, the mummified hand (amputated so long ago from the messages it was intended to transmit) said, "What's keeping you? Your flying carpet awaits!" Come back and dream in your lofty retreat, expand your consciousness — if it is true, as Cioran said, that:

> Consciousness was born in moments of freedom and laziness. As you lie down stretched out on the ground, your eyes staring at the sky above, the separation between you and the world opens up like a gap — without which consciousness is not possible.[11]

---

11. Emile M. Cioran, *Tears and saints*, translated by Ilinca Zarifopol-Johnston. University of Chicago Press, Chicago: 1995; p. 31.

Turn on the light, and close the curtains

In 1929, in an era when the situation of women still did not allow them much independence (although improved since 1859, when Michelet published *Woman*), Virginia Woolf was asked to give a talk on women and the novel. In the extraordinary meditation that is *A Room of One's Own*, rather than outlining and analyzing those literary productions, she chose to examine the conditions available to any female who wished to write: "A woman must have money and a room of her own if she is to write;"[12] especially if she wishes to write a work of fiction. In terms of money, Woolf posits that the minimum necessary would be some £500 per month, which must not result from an alienating and degrading job like those that were available to women at the time:

"Before that I had made my living by cadging odd jobs from newspapers, by reporting a donkey show here or a wedding there; I had earned a few pounds by addressing envelopes, reading to old ladies, making artificial flowers, teaching the alphabet to small children in a kindergarten. Such were the

---

12. Virginia Woolf, *A Room of One's Own*. Harcourt Brace Jovanovich, New York: 1957; p. 4.

chief occupations that were open to women before 1918."[13] Under the circumstances, her pathetic wages — earned by restraining and under-employing her faculties, filled her with hatred for her employers; she became bitter and obsessed with revenge. This material freedom was so hard won that it required complete forfeiture of independence of mind. Money obtained at this cost does not generate internal peace — that high degree of incandescence that, to Virginia Woolf, is the "non-material freedom" without which no work of fiction would ever see the light of day. (This is a point that she returns to many times, in that supple manner, like someone taking a casual stroll, that she uses in describing and reflecting upon the two days that preceded her speech.) She came to this conclusion, which became almost her watchword: *£500 per month, and a room of one's own.* Having your own room is a decisive step in gaining your freedom, but it is not enough. You still have to achieve a particular frame of mind, a lack of anxiety that sets you beyond resentment, anger and a desire to settle the score. The image of what you have had to overcome in order to achieve this must not encum-

---

13. *Ibid.*, p. 37.

ber you, it must not get inside you as an internalized obstacle — as the perpetuation of that torment of interruptions that constantly break a woman's train of thought. "If a woman wrote, she would have to write in the common sitting-room. And, as Miss Nightingale was so vehemently to complain, — 'women never have an half hour. . . that they can call their own' — she was always interrupted."[14]

A room of one's own — it was an unthinkable luxury for women in the past centuries to enjoy an uninterrupted block of time, to move in the continuum of a fully explored life of thought and imagination. (Woolf reminds us that Jane Austen and Charlotte Brontë wrote their novels without having any private space at all, without the knowledge of the people around them, and they even had trouble scraping together the money to buy paper.) When these favorable conditions come together, then material freedom and immaterial freedom coincide and the space of the room becomes one with the invaluable wisdom of Epictetus: focus on that which depends on us, in other words, "the things that are free, by nature, and avoid deterrence from men or obstruction from things" (*Handbook*).

14. *Ibid.*, p. 69-70.

The room is the empire of this non-dependence. It may be modest in size and decor, but nonetheless it represents a principle of invincibility — which is, actually, irreducible: the will to test our capabilities to their limits.

In her country house in Neauphle, where she spent long periods of solitude, Marguerite Duras used to host her friends for visits. When they would go out for a walk or went back home, she was alone again.

> I can recall the kind of silence there was after they went out. To enter that silence was like entering the sea. At once a happiness and a very precise state of abandonment to an evolving idea. A way of thinking or perhaps of not thinking — the two things are not so far apart. And also of writings."[15]

In the same work, which is so often considered to be an extension of Virginia Woolf's meditation, Marguerite Duras sees *A Room of One's Own* as establishing a new paradigm, laying a new foundation, a book whose immense influence on women and non-existent influence on men draws a dividing line between the sexes.

---

15. Marguerite Duras, *Practicalities*, translated from the French by Barbara Bray. William Collins, London: 1990; p. 43.

Because my room is just that — the space for that which is up to me — I change it as often as I like. I take down my posters and pin them to different walls. I am not bound to these walls. I move to different buildings, different neighborhoods; I move around in Paris. And every time, the room begins with me.

I find this mobility exalting. I leave just in order to leave. I come very close to the freedom of being indifferent, to its flaming absurdity. But no one room exactly resembles another. Their specific characteristics justify the excitement that comes from being in an unfamiliar place. These details include the direction they face and variations in the shape, size and height of the windows (I learned that an opening to the outdoors that is so high up that a person cannot reach it, and which is legally liable to be blocked up, is called "un jour de souffrance" — "a light of sufferance"), nuances in the color of the wallpaper, variations in the slope of the ceiling (you can't even stand upright in some attic rooms), the flooring — planks or tiles — and technical aberrations like a certain water tap that sounded like a ringing telephone when I shut off the water — as if it was trying to discretely remind me to do something. But they are no different in atmosphere, in the coloring of the soul. These rooms never offered anything more than temporary refuges (even if whole lives were lived out in them); walking into them, you don't feel that you are going into anyone's place in particular. They are the opposite of houses, rooted in generations of history, with their ghosts and all the desperate confessions, all the follies and secrets that their thick walls hold. Virginia Woolf knew how to listen in.

> The rooms differ so completely; they are calm or thunderous; open on to the sea, or, on the contrary, give on to a prison yard; are hung with washing; or alive with opals and silks; are hard as horsehair or soft as feathers — one has only to go into any room in any street for the whole of that extremely complex force of femininity to fly in one's face. How should it be otherwise? For women have sat indoors all these millions of years, so that by this time the very walls are permeated by their creative force.[16]

The rooms we lived in as students are not impregnated with our creative force. We don't stay in them long enough and, in any event even supposing

16. Virginia Woolf, *op. cit.*, p. 91.

that such a force exists, for the moment we leave it aside... We use it in other ways, and we squander it merrily. Later, no doubt, we will regret that; but even then, we will cherish in our memories the names of all those bars where we threw ourselves into animated, meaningless activity, the intense and fundamental futility of having nothing to do, so happily wasting our time... Places like the Bar des Oiseaux, de la Nuit, des Amis, de l'Avenir, des Savants, des Sportifs, du Progrès, des Philosophes, de la Moustache, de la Flottile, de la Marine, des Amarres, de la Patache, de la Passerelle, the Bar du Sud, du Nord, de l'Univers, de la Licorne; and cafés, like the Turin, the Madrid, the Amsterdam, the café de la Plage, de la Gare, d'En Face, de la Jetée, du Soleil, des Amériques, des Négociants, des Amateurs, and the Café des Artistes, des Voyageurs, des Folies, du Siècle, the Café de la Musique, the Tout Va Mieux, Les Deux Garçons, Les Deux Princes, Les Trois Diables, à la Fronde, au Florian, au Régent, à la Vielleuse, au Trianon, au Temps Perdu, au Lapin Agile, Chez Alice...

Bars and cafés are where we go to hunt for the phantom of liberty.

No children

Student life, with its halcyon days without deadlines, is a stark contrast to what adulthood — which supposedly brings awareness of real values — is supposed to bring: a life built on a horror of the void, of the least unfilled timeslot, a life stuffed to the breaking point with duties, jobs, responsibilities, chores, plans (you *have* a future and you manage it). There is always a way to squeeze more in; days are made of extraordinarily flexible stuff. You can seize the moment, starting at dawn and, proving your efficiency, use breakfast for business networking or a political meeting (why not restore the French royal ceremony of the "Lever"* — then we can start the public day even earlier), and from there on, everything else unfolds naturally, at full speed, until long into the night.

The goal is to outdo yourself, to get the better of your fatigue either by ignoring it completely, inuring yourself to the signals your body sends (not to listen to yourself, as they say), or by claiming that tiredness

---

*The French king's wake-up ceremony; certain nobles were invited to be present while his personal activities of the morning were performed, thus giving them the earliest possible access to the royal ear.

is our best ally, that tension, stress and nervousness add up to a terrific cocktail that stirs the blood and the imagination. *Workaholics*: fatigue is bigger than they are, and they have to load themselves up with files, they have to invent productive forms of insomnia. They have to, because if they stop for an instant, they collapse. And, indeed, they are pitiful in the rare moments when they are forced to stop working. Sometimes it happens because they find themselves someplace where working is not allowed — at the opera, for example, where they struggle in vain against their crushing exhaustion. As soon as the first notes of *Cosi fan tutte* are sounded, they fall into a black hole, and only crawl out of it when the theater erupts in applause.

Sometimes they give in because they really cannot help it anymore: it is a strange spectacle, at various hours of the night, to see whole train cars full of wiped-out businessmen. In their comas, they meet with lovers whom they never knew. I watch them and ask myself what I am doing there, the only one awake in the midst of these worn out troops that are being repatriated as fast as possible to their beds. And how much of this time in the express train do they remember? Nothing, or almost nothing. Transit time is an interruption in their planning, a lapse in the meeting preparations, the surprise of a different climate when the plane touches down at the end of the world. A sudden sweat soaks their armpits, running down their shirts and jackets. It streams down their faces, cascading around the eyes and in the ears. They feel lost and, instead of focusing on the three key points of their upcoming presentation to the president, they are liable to weird, contradictory desires — to bite into a frosty watermelon, or a hot piece of flesh...

In any case, even a full life, life lived at 200 miles an hour, must come to a halt one day. Some Monday morning comes along when you no longer have to go to your office (when somebody else's name plate is put up) and when, for every week and every month to come, the pages of your calendar are blank. This fatal Monday is coming closer and closer, since they keep reducing the retirement age. Trying to visualize the future and sure that women would soon be equal to men, at work, Virginia Woolf thought that it would reduce women's life expectancy, that they would die early, like men. (While she saw the future

of women as a harmonious progression, in fact several women coexist inside each one of us, and they
relate to disparate eras, some of them very archaic. A
woman can hold an important job without that taking anything away from the position of innate, absolute superiority that she accords to men in her private life, as the sole repositories of her happiness.)
Things have taken a different course, as we know.
Women do have access to a wider sphere of jobs, but
the conditions have changed. As a result, both sexes
find themselves ejected from active life, and a pro-
longed phase of inactivity opens out before them. At
this point in time, the things we learned as college
students, what they indirectly prepared us for and
what is their true value, now come into their own.
Wandering through books and through the world, a
taste for making new friends wherever we go, chance
encounters and conversations that can go on forever,
a deepening sense of self-love that instinctively lies
at the heart of childhood games. . . it is now that all
these "talents", picked up haphazardly, as a supple-
ment (if not an obstacle) to our formal studies and
career preparation, start to look as though they may
be what is most important, after all, without which

you cannot enjoy anything, especially given that at the end of the road we wind up back in our youth, in a comedy in which we are forced to go on vacation, and a major vacation at that.

As Nietzsche said, about the mania for planning:

> To make plans and project designs brings with it many good sensations; and whoever had the strength to be nothing but a forger of plans his whole life long would be a very happy man: but he would occasionally have to take a rest from this activity by carrying out a plan — and then comes the vexation and the sobering up,"[17]

Once I went to take a walk on the Promenade des Anglais, in Nice (where a plaque used to hang, next to the opera house at 26, rue Saint-François-de-Paul, saying: "Friedrich Nietzsche and his tormented genius lived in this house from 1865-1866"). Everywhere, on every bench and chair, old people sat facing the sea. They would try floating a few lines of conversation, but nothing seemed to catch on. Silence pretty much prevailed. Was it because of their long hours of contemplation of the blue expanse, where

---

17. Friedrich Nietzsche, *Human, All Too Human*, first part of the second volume published under the title *Assorted Opinions and Maxims*, translated by R. J. Hollingdale. Cambridge University Press, New York: 1986; p. 231.

their resistance to doing nothing, their last inclinations toward activity, just dissolved? Sitting there, in
the front row, above the waves, rocked by a soft, continuous Wagnerian music made by the rollers breaking upon themselves, these people seemed over-
whelmed by a splendor that was beyond them.

I shouldn't quite say that no conversation was
taking place at all. There were two inexhaustible
topics. One was the deplorable behavior of young
people today — their children and grandchildren.
Judgments about them were moderate, but generally
negative. It was not so much the children themselves
that were disappointing, but rather the wives or hus-
bands that they had chosen. It was them, the outsid-
ers, who led good kids astray. And it was with them,
alas! that they were having children of their own.
What painful lists of wrongs suffered, what endless
recitations of useless sacrifices. There, on the Promenade des Anglais, with the infinite sea before them
and inside of them their cruelly finite past, they re-
cited in a thousand variations, each one more sordid
than the last, Balzac's *Le Père Goriot*. Stories of sacri-
fice leave a bitter taste unless they are borne in a
deeply religious spirit. However, most of these parents who were so resentful at having been forsaken,

at having not been loved enough, did not have a strong religious faith. So they would start over, each one on his own account — but in the full certainty that on all the other benches, the same sad tales and the same long streams of griefs were being distilled.

I sat on the beach. A woman came over to me, just to tell me how her miserly daughter-in-law had schemed to have her driven out of her own house, in Brittany. Noticing that her story did not upset me, she went on the attack: "And you? Are you satisfied with your children? Do you get along well with them?" "I don't have any children." (Silence, and a long look.) — "That must be terrible", she said, and turned her back on me.

I don't have any children. A simple little sentence, but when you state it matter-of-factly, in passing (someone asks me, I answer) — the way you might say "I don't speak Portuguese" — it has the magical ability to put a chill in the air — the mute verdict of obsolete reprobation. The women around you start to look at you differently. How is that — you don't have any children? You're not a mother? You never wanted to have a baby? How can that be?! Every woman wants a baby. It's instinctive, the fulfillment of her nature. A woman without a child is an incomplete woman. She hardly deserves the name; we should invent some other term for this unnatural creature. Look at the movie stars, they want it all, the career and the baby: a baby, right away. And soon thereafter, three children. To launch a comeback: a baby, a film, and a novel.

I still remember the words of a doctor who was irritated at having to be an accessory to a woman who was so little concerned with her reproductive capabilities. "Aren't you tired of taking contraceptives?" No, I was not tired. Not at all. I even thought that the pill tasted good. On the other hand, I believed (and it was up to me, after all, to assess my own powers of endurance), that I would be very tired indeed if I tried to raise a family. Each one has his or her weak point. Obviously, despite being a specialist in the human body, the doctor was one of those innumerable people who, as Philippe Muray observed,[18] confuse women's genitals and their wombs. He didn't want to hear any more; and I didn't want to say anything more. How can I defend myself against the hostility that seems to combine in some confused way

---

18. "Why," I asked him, "do they always use the word 'womb' in this context? I'm starting to get sick of it." "Which context?" "Uh, well, in erotic dialogue. In the middle of direct, sexually explicit conversation. When talk about procreation is most out of place," Philippe Muray, *Postérité*, Paris, Grasset, 1988, p. 52-53.

the law of the species and the commandments of religion, and the approbation of the media? What
could I say? That nothing in that whole business ever
appealed to me, neither the pregnancy, the childbirth,
nor the daily requirements of feeding a child, of taking care of it, of raising it? That the idea of a love that
would spring up so automatically and last for so long
(with every chance of outliving me) disturbed me?
That I didn't have any energy for something that is
likely to go on forever, for something that allowed no
room for the fluctuating moods of the heart? I could
also say that I lived in too small an apartment, that I
moved too often. That I had no inclination toward
marriage and a non-existent sense of responsibility.
That I am egoistical, infantile, and far too busy having
fun to take any interest in another person's games.
That I never felt the connection between my desire
for a man and having a child. I didn't see the link.

And maybe it also has to do with my phobia, as a
child, of being interrupted by my parents? Later, I
looked around and noticed that my view had been
shortsighted. I did see some young children with
mothers: and they interrupted them all the time!
Fragmented time, actually, that's the life of a mother
with children. And it takes considerable skill and dis-

cretion to hide how exhaustingly repetitive and alienating such work is. As Marguerite Duras wrote about
the woman at home,

> She has to make her time-table conform to those
> of other people — her own family and the various
> organizations it's connected with. . . . From the
> man's point of view a woman is a good mother
> when she turns this discontinuity into a silent and
> unobtrusive continuity.[19]

You'll see, my mother used to say — when your turn
comes, when you have children. Well, I didn't see. I
skipped my turn.

I keep quiet. I have nothing to say, no convinc-
ing reason. It's not important to me to win a following on this matter. It's just not that important.
Women without children keep quiet, in contrast to
the endless chatter from mothers and about mothers,
to the omnipresence of the Virgin and Child.

These words are spoken by both women and
men, either in adoration or blasphemy, execration —
but always vehemently. Those who rail against
mothers, those who worship sterility, thunder from
their soapboxes: Swift, Sade, Schopenhauer,
Nietzsche, Thomas Bernhard, Kundera. . . They speak

---

19. Marguerite Duras, *op. cit.*, p. 45.

for themselves or for their works, against a power of fertility that is foreign for them. They take an intense and desperate stance vis-à-vis Woman. In their desire to escape the Law of the Species, they use any tool that comes to hand, any argument, even if it's misogynist. Their goal is to save the unique, absolute quality of their existence, of their creation.

A woman who rejects the maternal role is less excited, verbally — less philosophical and declamatory. She is a weak advocate for her cause and a minority within her own gender; feeling allegiance to her kind, she cannot place Woman in the role of Enemy. When it comes to men, and questioning their desire to be fathers, to procreate, then sometimes it's appropriate and necessary to speak up, but this seldom leads to tirades intended to apply universally. A man who does not want a child says "No" to the other person, to his beloved, who is suddenly changed into an adversary whose beauty and tears are liable to make him give in. A woman who does not want a child says "No" for herself, and her refusal, while often inaudible or not articulated at all, is beyond appeal. It's only an ellipsis. A decisive touch of negativity in a life plan, an homage to the spirit of rupture.

WAYS OF TRAVELING

In those student years, dedicated to the art of loving and living without a future, traveling seemed to me to be the only possible vocation; here was an activity whose goal was so vast that it exceeded the resources of a lifetime. It could never be tiresome or boring! There was to see so much, why bother to learn a trade, why build your own prison? I did not understand the obstinate injunction that we should foreclose our future under the pretext of forging weapons by which we might master it. It was enough, it seemed to me, to simply get going.

Now, many are the ways that one may travel. And, as opposed to what I naively believed when I wanted to make it my "profession", it's not the num-

ber of miles crossed that counts. I'll draw some dis-
tinctions between the different ways, because in
writing, as in space, we advance linearly; but they all
combine and meld together fluidly, in fact. And there
is something in us, sometimes a hiker, sometimes an
explorer, a fugitive, or an adventurer, who dominates
and leads the way.

Walking — and walking away

It's a shame that we can't remember the first
time we were able to walk — the day when the world
stopped being limited to the arched top of a cradle,
the smooth expanse of a ceiling, the foliage of a
tree — and opened out before us, inviting us to explore it on our own and suddenly seeming endless.
The day I learned to swim, while it's almost as long
ago as the first, is so clear in my mind that I not only
can still tell the story, but I get an acute sense of
amazement and revelation every time I go swimming:
I float, and as I watch the aqua waves get deeper, they
no longer threaten to overcome me — the deeper they
get, the better they support me.

The act of walking, of going out for a stroll, doesn't

reactivate the miraculous moment when we learned to walk (except at certain moments of grace, or after a long disease, when it's stunning to be on our feet again, outdoors). Maybe that's why writings about taking a walk or, in a novel, about the way a character walks, have always caught my attention. They snap us out of our complacency. They remind us that it was an achievement, and that how we exercise it is a vital aspect of how we live. Like the discovery of pre-historic cave paintings, everything that revives lost memories in us, that recalls a time before an acquired knowledge was taken for granted — being able to talk, for example — is appealing.

Learning a foreign language is always a powerful experience. It gives us access to something unknown: new friendships, books, cities, a whole country; and at the same time, it recalls a chaotic and obscure background: the dizzying swirl of unfamiliar sounds, the will to understand, breakthroughs and then sudden breakdowns into confusion and complete discouragement, when no gleam of progress can be seen and we think we will be condemned to stammer forever.

The German philosopher Karl Gottlob Schelle

claims, in *L'Art de se promener* [*The Art of Taking a Walk*] to have achieved a wisdom and an ideal of happy sociability. As a partisan of a popular philosophy, Schelle is astonished that humanity puts so much intellectual energy into posing and investigating abstract problems, so far removed from its daily needs and the scope of its existence, while showing no curiosity, no philosophical interest, in what concerns it closely — as if thought, in its purest form, could not be related to questions of use of time, food, sleep, solitary and community activities, physical and mental harmony, as if intelligence were not above all the ability to organize the course of each day as well as possible (with all that that implies for how we organize our nights) and deciding how best to use our time, before launching out into abstract divagations.

There is a famous fable about a philosopher who falls into a hole because he is looking up at the stars. Do we really have to choose between what is high and what is low, the abstract and the concrete, the mind and the body, philosophy and the world? If we paid full attention to the art of living as the peak of our reflexive and creative possibilities, would that not have the power to reconcile what schooling and tradition artificially separate and allow us the fullest range of exploration? If one is sure of his balance, and knows the terrain, he can consider the heavens and the constellations without breaking a leg. One can even use the light of the stars to help him avoid obstacles. We can take inspiration from the art of the tightrope walker, and strive to emulate his flexibility, his dancing step between the earth and sky.

It's no coincidence that the first chapter of *Thus Spoke Zarathustra* tells the story of the funambulist, the acrobat, who made "danger his trade". But that is going far beyond the hygienic and ethical concerns of Schelle, for whom the walker never leaves the solid ground. "In an art of living that alternates effort with rest, serious undertakings and play-time, work and pleasure, going for a walk also has its place."[1] Schelle launches into a praise of walking, both for its physical benefits (the body vitally needs movement) and for its intellectual value: outside the confinement of the room, the mind is released from methodical and rigorous reflection, and opens up to meditation along a course that follows the whims of the spectacle that

1. Karl Gottlob Schelle, *L'Art de se promener*, foreword and French translation by Pierre Deshusses, Paris, Payot & Rivages, Petite Bibliothèque, 1996, p. 24.

comes into view. "While taking a walk, don't force yourself to concentrate; it should be more of a game than a serious effort. Your mental attention should slip over the objects, to some extent, responding to their invitations rather than being forced to study them."[2] The walker is an expert at suspended atten-tion, enjoying the appearances of things. Without a specific goal, he lets images come to him randomly — details, fragments, or a panoramic vision — that draw him into a daydream, giving his thoughts unforeseen resonance. He dreams and thinks at the same time; the two currents are intertwined, which is one of the considerable charms of taking a walk.

In order to enhance the freedom of this pleasure, it is important to choose your location well. In a small town where everyone knows everyone else, it is impossible to give in and the "let the spirit run free", because everyone we meet is linked to our past and reasserts the existing definitions of ourselves. In a big city, on the other hand, we are more likely to come across something unforeseen. And, even if we have lived there all our lives, it does not become ba-nal. There is always something more to discover.

---

2. *Ibid.*, p. 33.

However, even the big city is not enough for Schelle. It will always be an integral part of our network of concerns; it controls our flow of thoughts too directly. For Schelle, only nature will do, because "the grandeur and freedom of nature release us from the petty contingencies imposed by the townsman's yoke."[3] But what kind of nature? If we take our counselor's advice, we will avoid the extremes. Too flat a landscape dulls the senses and plunges us into somnolence, while the dramatic vistas of the mountain are too striking. Admittedly, they wake us up, but they stimulate us too much, and between exaltation and terror, the heart has no more room for serenity. And leaving the lofty summits to refresh ourselves by the banks of a rushing stream is even worse:

"Because of the enormous masses of water, which are always oppressive to the soul, which obstruct the freedom of the heart"![4] Schelle cautions against the sublime. "Who would not like to walk alone in the midst of the Alps?", he asked. Then in which direction would we set out — not to make the heart beat wildly and not, in our desire to be "completely by ourselves", to allow nature to obsess

3. *Ibid.*, p. 48.
4. *Ibid.*, p. 93.

us with its power (which is exactly what happens in the streets we know, where we are usually preoccupied by the familiar faces we meet)? Schelle suggests the mellow valleys which, without stifling us, give the impression of "protecting us from the rest of the world."

Schelle's ideal of nature is, fundamentally, an immense garden, not over-populated at all, and whose boundaries remain invisible to us. It is Eden. The euphoria of the walker brings him back to the era before sin. To be really liberating, going for a walk supposes that you are open to yourself, and preserve a certain state of innocence. "If the person is considered, the first condition necessary to the walk is a certain ingenuousness of the heart."[5] It is only at this price that the walker can saunter merrily along, open to the vagaries of memory, in a pure state of awareness of the present. The art of walking inclines us, according to Schelle, toward a certain quality of the heart. And it is to attain that serene unconcern that he gives so many recommendations: he invites us not to read while walking, he advises against using a walk to facilitate digestive processes (the body's slug-

---

5. *Ibid.*, p. 41.

gishness is detrimental to spiritual flight) and thinks it is reasonable not to force one's physical stamina: fatigue is a negative influence. That means that early morning walks are out: "What are most advantageous for the body and the spirit are walks in midmorning in the summer-time, if they are not too tiring."[6]

As for the question of solitude, he recommends not overdoing it there, either. He appreciates solitary walks, for he considers that taking a walk by yourself is primarily a way of conversing with yourself and, in this dialogue, "letting yourself be surprised by yourself". But, as it is not only surprise that helps us, a friend might be welcome to come along. And it seems that this wisdom, dispensed step by step, serves as a safeguard. "To walk is a free pleasure, it cannot coexist with any constraint,"[7] wrote Schelle; but, perhaps because he knows all too well that the freedom of walking is virtually unlimited, he tries to set some boundaries, to confine it within the scope of pleasure and entertainment. Schelle, who knew his Rousseau, criticizes the latter's inability to simply skim over the spectacle of the world and to be satisfied with its

---

6. *Ibid* p. 129.
7. *Ibid*, p. 42.

shimmer. He rejects the violence of Rousseau's moods, the fanatical insistence on solitude and the radical asociality that lie at the heart of Rousseau's vision of the walk. He disapproves of the excessive passion, verging on hysteria.

This prudent attitude did not prevent Schelle from losing his mind at a very young age. And so it was, essentially, between the four walls of an asylum that he would go on to practice his art of walking. Or was it that very prudence that made him lose his mind — in contrast to those exalted ones who stride with impunity, taking giant steps far from beyond known landmarks, where the air is sharpest, and without bothering to take the ways of Reason.

For Rousseau, as the beautiful title of *Reveries of a Solitary Walker* says so well, any true walk is solitary. The first lines of that astonishing monologue reiterate it (lines that are striking, among other reasons, in the manner by which the author succeeds in making the monomania that is eating away at him appear tempt-ing — equipping it with an irresistible musical qual-ity, in enrolling us in the Club of his obsessions, and imparting to us the dream of insularity that obsesses him). Not as a temporary spell of solitude in a life that is grounded in society, but as an awakening of a state of chronic, irremediable loneliness.

But, curiously, the more Rousseau tries to build up the despair of such total loneliness, which so unjustly fell upon him, "the most sociable and loving person, the one who most enjoyed human beings", the more one feels welling up, at the pace of an indefatigable marcher, the inverse — the joy that goes with such dereliction — and the better we understand that it is, in fact, a divine pleasure to be liberated from the others: from the Parisian social clubs, the deafening echo chamber of salon conversations, the militancy of the *Encyclopédistes*, the dust of books.

> One of my greatest joys was above all to leave my books safely shut up and to have no escritoire. . . . Instead of all these gloomy old papers and books, I lilled my room with flowers and grasses."[8]

"All wrapped up in himself," Rousseau devoted himself to that "precious *far niente*." It was, he wrote,

> . . . my first and greatest pleasure, and I set out to

8. Jean-Jacques Rousseau, *Reveries of the Solitary Walker*, translated by Peter France. Penguin Books, New York: 1979; p. 83-84.

taste it in all its sweetness, and everything I did
during my stay there was in fact no more than the
delectable and necessary pastime of a man who
has dedicated himself to idleness.[9]

Rousseau's isolation is irremediable because he
wants it that way, because it is his means of escaping
a philosophical and strategic setting that conflicts
with his own genius and that would keep him from
fully plumbing the depths of his own mind, in fear
and rapture, with all the surprises that it holds for
him. (Similarly, when Nietzsche gives up his post as
professor at the University of Basle at the age of 34
and begins a wanderer's life, he certainly has to give
in to the constraints of illness but, more profoundly,
he gives himself the conditions necessary for free
thought; he allows for the unburdening, the uproot-
ing, that are indispensable to self-knowledge.) Rousseau, a past master in self-love, an expert in irrespon-
sibility in all its forms, was never mistaken as to
where his own good might lie. And the *Reveries of a
Solitary Walker* emanate from this secret knowledge,
the touchstone of a peculiar freedom (never acknowl-
edged since, within his own system, Rousseau occu-

---

9. *Ibid*, p. 83.

pies the place of the victim, the one who is not in a position to choose) — a testamentary text that was never finished, like a walk that one set out on without any intention of returning.

Just setting out is all it takes: just walking straight ahead, lost in your own thoughts, deaf to any calls for you to pay attention. That is how Rousseau liberated himself from Geneva, long before the escape from Paris that opened the door on the great phase of his creative maturity. He left behind him the mediocrity of his unsuccessful studies and the false attachment of people who did not love him. Or rather — and the technique of projecting onto others is already recognizable here — it is Geneva that shut him out. It was not up to him. He wanted to re-enter the city, but the gate was closed; so the young man had no choice anymore but to continue on his way. This is more a philosophy of marching than strolling. When you go out for a stroll, you come back. When you walk away, you may never come back. The energy and the thrill that swirl in your head, then, bring a risk and a desire not to stop. Without saying it, perhaps even without having noticed it, the walker leaves the streets of his own neighborhood, gets through the entire park, and goes past the last house at the edge of town. This is not the gentle gait of the casual stroll, with a pause on a bench, a benevolent glance at the surroundings. This protagonist has caught the fever of the vagabonds, the faith of pilgrims. He has launched himself on a voyage with no return. Thus, in *Walking*, Henry David Thoreau (an enthusiastic disciple of Rousseau) wrote: "Our expeditions are but tours, and come round again at evening to the old hearth-side from which we set out. Half the walk is but retracing our steps. We should go forth on the shortest walk, perchance, in the spirit of undying adventure, never to return, — prepared to send our embalmed hearts only as relics to our desolate kingdoms. If you are ready to leave father and mother, brother and sister, wife and child and friends, and never to see them again, — if you have paid your debts, and made your will, and settled all your affairs , and are a free man, then you are ready for a walk."[10]

The walker, according to Rousseau and Thoreau, does not take anyone along. Like the people who stroll through Thomas Bernhard's novels, he takes the opposite direction, he goes *against*. His art

10. Henry David Thoreau, *Walking*, Applewood Books, Bedford, MA, 1992, pp. 6-7.

of walking is not a matter of relaxation, or health. It is an act of independence, a declaration of insubordination. Thoreau, although at first he was undecided, not knowing which way his steps would take him, always ends up going toward the west — toward the rougher ground, toward what does not yet exist. Against Europe: its urban landscape, its culture, its coded intelligence, its analytical refinement. He allows himself to be guided by that which is still unknown within himself. And if the world where he walks is never wild enough for his liking, that is because he seeks the wilderness in correspondence with a spiritual anarchy — with a part of himself that has been left fallow voluntarily: the part of him that chose not "The Society for the Dissemination of Useful Knowledge" but "The Society for the Dissemination of Useful Ignorance".

Writing and traveling: Flaubert in the Orient

The inverse of this departure-as-a-rupture, this heading off toward the desert — a negative initiatory voyage that serves as a gesture of revolt — is the positive initiatory voyage, a formative experience from which one hopes to return enriched by experiences and memories. In this case, writing and traveling are, ideally, two supposedly complementary actions, mutually fostering each other in a kind of energetic optimism that is pumped back and forth from the knee to the wrist and back, as if the desire to see the world and traverse it were only an extension of a desire to write, a desire that would feed on metaphorical changes of scene, attractive images, fascinating whims. Between image and mirage, the perspective of language (like that of nature) can only provide an approximation, so that the result inevitably falls a little short of what was experienced. But this very disappointment is what re-energizes the traveler-writer, exhausted but reinvigorated, who always recharges himself with that inaccessible source that supports the perseverance of the man who walks as well as the man who writes. (Whenever you travel, people who write crop up everywhere — in waiting rooms, trains, the coffee shop, at the shore. At the inn, in the blue shade of the Virginia creeper, they are describing the blue shade of the Virginia creeper, and the inn, on their lined notepads. When the waitress sets a glass on the table, they do not look up. You cannot see and, at the same time, have seen.)

This ardor to transcribe, however, is deeply intermingled with a tendency to be distracted. Unfinished books, interminable roads: the lack of an ending allows you to stop wherever you wish, but also, more secretly, to start up and to go on advancing — advancing and getting lost. There is nobody to show you the way. There is no objective regulator. It all takes place in the solitary excitement between words and visions, continuing endlessly but without urgency, changing and continuous, from the blank page to the spectacle of the world, and back. Traveling makes writers of us; and the writer who travels enters a special state of blankness, during which he is momentarily but wholly available. And while it may seem that he is wasting time (if there seems to be a cost), it is only in order to accumulate material that will contribute to his future work. This is a subtle and well-considered economics that is clearly at work in Flaubert's correspondence during his travels in the Orient. The "local color" is recognized as a precious substance, pure, unadulterated with familiar or European elements — the substance of strangeness that one strives to assimilate while preserving its definitively remote character.

The traveler creates, in mental and sensual terms, a collection of living tableaux that he will seek to bring back to his country, sparkling with the incomprehension in which they appeared to him. He may allow himself to appear in these pictures, but only marginally (a silhouette at the foot of a pyramid, a pensive subject perched on a camel or lounging on the back of a giant tortoise), in order to authenticate and show how essentially exotic they are. Poses are chosen to highlight the impossibility of actually fitting oneself into such a scene. This is the source of the astonishment, curiosity, admiration, and deep melancholy, when the image tends to envelop the traveler and threaten to obliterate his identity. The spleen of forbidden coitus... Flaubert wrote to Louis Bouilhet: "March 13, 1850, on board our *cange*, 12 miles out from Syène.... Just imagine, my friend, five or six winding streets with houses approximately four feet high, built of dried gray mud. In the doorways, women stand, or sit on braided mats. These Negresses wear sky blue dresses, or yellow, white, red.... The scent of spices flows through; and on the women's throats we see long collars of gold piastres, which jingle like cart bells when they move. They call to us with trailing voices: *Cawadja, cawadja*; their white teeth shine under their red and black lips; their eyes of tin roll like wheels turning. . . . Top off this scene with a brilliant sun. Ah well: I did not go with any of them. . . purposely, I stood apart, in order to preserve the melancholy of this tableau and to allow it to penetrate more deeply into my mind's eye. Therefore I left feeling completely bedazzled, a feeling that is still with me now. There is nothing more lovely than these women calling to you. If I had gone with them, another image would have overlaid that one and would have attenuated its splendor."

This account reminds me of another, similar one. I have retained just as clear an image of it, and nothing has intervened to diminish its brilliance. I am walking in the prostitutes' district in Bombay. Lacking a room, some make love behind a curtain hung in the street. I happen to cross the line of sight of a girl leaning out a window. Before I really see her, she throws a rotten mango in my face. Maybe she shouts something at me. But I'm not paying attention to that; I'm taking in the melancholic atmosphere.

Travelers, male or female, never come back without images, whether splendid or sordid. And that is true precisely because they come back. In the course they follow while they are abroad and which they narrate in the letters that keep them in regular contact with their point of origin, no matter how far they go, it is the return that is being crafted, built and animated by the thousand tales that go into it. The journey has only one goal: the return. As this sentence from one of Diderot's letters to Sophie Volland testifies, time becomes unreal, during the journey, distorted by the future anterior: "I will have completed the most marvelous possible voyage when I am back" (from Saint Petersburg, December 29, 1773). From Paris, when he had not yet left his home turf, Flaubert wrote to his mother: "I will tell you wonderful travel tales, we will wander in the desert as we sit by the fire; I will tell you of my nights under the tent, my days under the bright sun. . . [And] we will say to ourselves: 'Oh! Do you remember how sad we were!' and we will hug each other, remembering our anguish at parting" (October 27, 1849). It is the absolute of this present moment, or these present interlocutors, that seals the journey and all it represents into the past, and through shared memories neutral-

izes the lure of somewhere else. Travel makes everyone a writer: goodbye, I'll write to you, I'll describe to
you the things that are separating us. The words in
the letter or the card will attempt to obliterate, tem-
porarily, the geographical distance and to make the
foreign place name more reassuring, or at least more
conceivable. This promise to correspond guarantees
that the distance is not significant and that there is
no need to fear any change of view that could fade the
image of home or of mother.

Thanks to the great number of his letters, almost
all of them addressed to his mother, we can follow
the continued progress of Flaubert's voyage from November 1849 to spring 1851, when he rejoined his
mother (who came to meet him in Venice). At first,
he was writing to help the old woman (who was already mourning her daughter) to endure his absence
and to give her the feeling that her son was still by
her side. That is, the letters were an attempt to declare that the countries traversed were of secondary
importance. The countries are just an anecdotal element that never surpasses the emotional function of
the letter: "Ah! poor mother, how I wish I could slip

into mine [my letters], between these folds of paper that I look upon with so much tenderness for you." The words of the letter replace, imperfectly, the loved one. The correspondence creates the fiction of a two-way movement of replacement or displacement. The traveler wants to put himself where his words are and thus to find himself back where he started his journey, to abolish the rift created by the journey, while the recipient, the person who did not go away, will use all the resources of his imagination to put himself where the traveler is. Flaubert gives plenty of advice. He encourages his mother to go to the Louvre to see the Assyrian bas-reliefs: "You can enjoy the thought that I am looking at similar carvings. Try, poor old mother, to put yourself in my place while I am away. Dream of the beautiful things that I will be seeing, how I will be gasping with delight at all the marvels." And, on the part of the traveler, what matters is not so much to see the world as to select extracts from it to dream upon, to use in prolonging the reveries of the days from before he left.

This is why notations about light are so essential. Light is the very element of the dream, and we enter it without putting up any resistance. "I saw the

Orient through, or rather in, a great silvery light melted on the sea," Flaubert wrote of his arrival in Alexandria. His voyage is a progression through the immaterial. The further he goes, the more Flaubert has the impression that he is finding something that had been missing, rather than discovering something new. And it is on a note of boredom and indifference that he concludes these long months in search of every possible form of exoticism (tanned and disguised in local garb, trying the local drugs and sexual conventions, including sodomy: "Traveling both for our own education and charged with a mission by the government, we saw it as our duty to make ourselves available for this mode of ejaculation" he wrote — not to his mother, this time, but to his friend Louis Bouilhet). And while Flaubert is so methodically experiencing the differences and visiting the strangest and most foreign spaces, at the same time he realizes that the only thing that has really occurred is that time has been passing. At the conclusion of this circular tour, Flaubert notes only that he has aged (like Zazie, in Queneau's book, when she is found 24 hours later at the Lyon train station, but on the departure side). With typical Flaubertian irony, this leads us to a definition of "the traveler", in *The Dictionary of Accepted Ideas*: Always "intrepid", as in, "Here, intrepid traveler, you may see. . ." And often substituted by "Ladies and gentlemen", the way they address people in organized tour groups.

Seeing, touching: Rimbaud's flight

Traveling with Rimbaud, we are far from the style of the commercial tour. When he runs away, there is another figure of the mother in the background, a very different one, and history leaves us this illustrative gesture: aged, and especially so in her own mind, weighted down with virginal mourning and marital rancor, Mme. Rimbaud permits herself the luxury of visiting the tomb that awaits her, between her two dead children, Vitalie and Arthur. A living rendition of the Pietà, the image of suffering itself, this is the specter that the foreign tourist flees, from port to port, and under whose eyes the prospect of going home takes on a macabre irony. "Before sealing the stone at the entrance, which we call a door, and which is fifty centimeters square, just enough room to get the coffin through, I wanted to visit it one more time, to see whether there was anything that needed to be done. The workmen gently slipped me all the way in to the back of the vault; some held me by the shoulders, and the others by the feet. Everything was as it should be, and that was the moment that I had the cross and the boxwood set in place. Getting out of the vault was harder, for it is very deep; but these men are very skilful, and pulled me up alright, though with difficulty" (Letter to her daughter, Isabelle, June 1, 1900). And it is true, as Mme. Rimbaud said: it is getting out of the tomb that is difficult. Unless you happen to have exceptionally skilful grave-diggers.

This scene of funereal devotion is a perfect window, according to the floating and irrefutable precision of oneiric logic, on the mute and cold sadness that colors the correspondence between Rimbaud and his mother. No joy flows from one to the other, nor even a voice. And if Mme. Rimbaud happens, long after the death of her son, to evoke some great emotion on his behalf, some inexplicable happiness, it is when she meets a young man at church whom she mistakes for "poor Arthur". He is missing a leg, and is very pious. She recognizes him first by his crutch.

Rimbaud started his life on the road by running away from home in September 1870, leading his mother to write, "The police are working to find out where he has gone, and I am very much afraid that by the time you receive this, that little fool will have been arrested once again; but he need not come home, for I swear that in my lifetime I will not take him back in anymore." Rather than a traveler, Rimbaud was a fugitive. That is, his various expeditions take on the negative connotations of truancy. Running away, unlike traveling, has nothing to do with the search for the picturesque, for the remote and exotic; it is the search for a place where one can rest, stop running, an end to flight, an end to the risk of being caught. Pleasure trips may be based on the assumption of a safe return, while running away marks a rupture that cannot be patched over by going back. Running away is a harsh, one-way trip, an anguish, without guide or interpreter.

From his province to Paris, then between England, Belgium, Holland, and Germany, etc., Rimbaud wandered around close to France, at first, before going farther and farther afield, gradually finding his way to Africa and Arabia. His trips — and his returns, which he saw as failures — make the family home the repulsive and at the same time inevitable center, where he would wash up, sick and demoralized, in order to renew his energy for a new departure in reaction against the death and the coldness that are, to him, synonymous with Charleville. "I am dying, I am rotting in the flatness, the unpleasantness, the dullness" (Rimbaud to his professor George Izambard, in November 1870). But the uneven pattern of his comings and goings from his mother's house would be drawn out until it became one long, extended line (which would be broken, if only by the paucity of communication links) between Harare and the Ardennes.

When he was about to set out on his first trip to Egypt, from Genoa, November 17, 1878, he wrote one of the longest and most descriptive letters in his correspondence. Indeed, this last letter from Europe represents a *passage* (the Mt. Saint Gothard pass); it is like a final trace of his writing before it is transformed into that blank space of an epistolary exchange where the characters of the recipient and the signatory have disappeared. And what this extremely lively and suggestive letter enables us to see precisely and even physically is the complete absence of visibility, the volume of opacity and night in which the path of the traveler is obliterated.

"Look! No more shadows above, below or around, although we are surrounded by enormous objects; no more road, precipice, gorge, nor sky: there is nothing to think, touch, see, or not see except this whiteness, for it is impossible to raise one's eyes from the white nuisance that one believes to be the middle of the path. Impossible to raise the nose to a north wind so lacerating, the eyelashes and moustache covered in stalactites, the ears in tatters, the neck swollen. Without the shadow that is oneself and without the telegraph poles, which follow the supposed road, we would be in as much trouble as a sparrow in an oven."

The snowstorm's merciless smothering of the world extended well beyond the Mt. Saint Gothard pass, throughout the rest of Rimbaud's voyages so regularly punctuated with negative notations. It's as if venturing into unknown territory revealed to us, most of all, the infinite expanse of all that which we no longer see. From Cyprus he writes: "There is nothing here but a chaos of rocks, the river and the sea. There is only one house. There is no cultivated plot, no garden, not a tree. In summer, it is 80 degrees." And later, from Aden: "Aden is a dreadful rock, without a blade of grass nor a drop of good water: they drink distilled sea water," or "it is the base of a volcano, with no plant life," or even "you cannot imagine what this place is like at all. There are no trees here, even desiccated ones, not a bit of grass, no plot of land, not a drop of fresh water. Aden is the crater of an extinct volcano, plus sand and the sea. So you don't see or touch absolutely anything here but lava and sand that cannot produce the least plant." The positive version of these descriptions in the few geographical reports that Rimbaud sent to French magazines: data on the territorial area, the altitude, the number and size of rivers, the seasons, names of the tribes, their gods, their flocks and their wild animals.

Snow and sand. The Alps and the Arabian desert come together to produce a space where thirst reigns. In this course of progressive natural rarefaction that accompanies the voyage, fresh water is the first element to be removed (at a way-station on the approach to Mt. Saint Gothard, says Rimbaud, a mug of salty water costs fifty francs).

Thirst and sweat — when traveling doesn't mean looking at but getting into violent hand-to-hand combat with the country being explored. This is not a collection of images but a physical test. Seeing and touching then become one and the same. The lack of colorful descriptions does not reflect indifference or insensitivity (even Flaubert admits, at the end of his voyage, that that is only the backdrop of reality against which the search for local color is launched), but a deepening of experience at the sensory level, in immediate contact, both defensive and aggressive, with the unknown. The vision that is developed here has nothing to do with remote choices, gratuitous amused glances. It is hard, desolate, *vital*. It is tied to the essence, to that without which one truly would perish. The last letter that Rimbaud dictated to his sister and that he left with the Marseille shipping director concludes with the lines, "I am completely paralyzed: therefore I wish to be onboard early." While leaving may be a bit like dying, dying is definitively *staying put*.

Intrepid traveler: Isabelle Eberhardt

"Reborn" is the word used by Isabelle Eberhardt every time she found herself back in North Africa — feeling prey to risk, again, and surrounded with mysteries, as reflected by the vast residence in a neighborhood on the outskirts of Tunis where she spent the summer of 1899 (at the age of 22).

> The house was a labyrinth of complicated corridors and rooms situated on different levels, decorated with old-fashioned, multicoloured faience. Plaster delicately carved in lacework bordered the arched wooden ceilings, which were painted and gilded.[11]

The girl lived alone there, with an old Moorish maidservant and a black dog named Daedalus. During the day, she would dream, lounging in the half-light of the cool rooms; at night, disguised as a Bedouin, she would wander in the labyrinth of streets and passageways. She walked through the Moslem cemeteries and prowled the port district, among the beggars and prostitutes.

For five more years, until she drowned (swept

---

11. Isabelle Eberhardt, *Prisoner of Dunes*, translated by Sharon Bangert. Peter Owen Publishers, London: 1995; p. 95.

away by a crude *wadi* — or assassinated, but there has
never been any evidence to support that hypothesis),
Isabelle Eberhardt never recoiled from any obstacle
that stood between her and the deep desert. With a
heroic, quasi-mystical resolution, she faced scandal,
disease, poverty, violent attacks. Never, even during
the hardest times in her life (which she sometimes
narrates as a male, sometimes as a female), did she
reconsider the certainty that drove her: she was
made for the precipice of departures, the wandering
life, adventurous audacity. She recognized that as her
vocation, her natural gift. The reality of this talent
shows up in her writings not as great narratives but
in the accumulation of moments, selected moments.
These are primarily the *apotheoses of the evening*, the
hour when the sun in Africa drops its fatal power and
blazes up in splendor; the *nights under the beautiful stars*
(in her marvelous simplicity, Eberhardt shares with
us the gesture of spreading a carpet and lying down
on it — in a street, the back room of a coffee house, a
courtyard, in the open desert, in the middle of that
strange marine landscape formed by the waves of
sand: "Slowly, gently, I fall asleep in the calm atmos-

phere of this shack whose door does not close, in the unguarded courtyard, out in the open in the *bled* ('upcountry') darkness. . . ," or: "We enjoyed a very sweet sleep under a broad pomegranate, in the dazzling sun that was already high in the sky. . ."; and *awakening*: "I felt the delicious taste of freedom, peace and well-being which, for me, always comes when I wake up amid the familiar spectacles of nomad life," and: "After a short lunar night spent on a mat in front of the Moorish coffee house of the *makhzen*, in the *ksar* (fortified village) of Beni-Ounif, I wake up happy, with the delicious feelings that always come to me when I have slept outdoors, under the open sky, and when I am about to take to the road again." And, reading her, we understand that these moments that cost her so much hardship were well worth her trouble, that she may have faced all these dangers just for the private joys of waking up that way.

About a visit to Marseille, Isabelle Eberhardt wrote,

> I had passed through this great city of departures many times. . . wearing borrowed costumes chosen to suit the place and circumstance. Dressed

as a young European woman I would never have
seen anything; the world would have been closed
to me, for external life seems to have been made for
man and not for woman.[12]

Dressing up as a man keeps Eberhardt from being locked into any one personality. "In male clothing
and a borrowed personality, I camped then in the
douar of the *caïdat* of Monastir, in the company of Si
Elarrhby, *khalifa*. The young man never suspected that
I was a woman. He called me his brother Mahmoud
and I shared his wandering life and his work for two
months." At that time, she was Si Mahmoud Saâdi, a
little Turk who had run away from school in France.
But she had other identities, under which she spent
nights in a brothel and drinking, with the Foreign
Legion, in cafés with exotic names like Béchar's
Return, Star of the South, The Soldier's Mother,
Figuig Oasis. . .

For Eberhardt, exile and freedom were one and
the same thing. She had a passion for danger. Her
drugs of choice were hashish, opium, *kif* and remote
places. And, of course, nothing was ever enough. Sitting in a bar on the *rive gauche* in Paris, Guy Debord

---

12. *Ibid.*, p. 59.

discovered more than complete intoxication, "the real taste of time passing". Eberhardt buried herself in the Country of Sand to experience "the infinite duration of what is". How incalculable is the internal distance traveled by a voyager.

The nothingness of tourism

Flaubert's search for the exotic (which reproduces on a much vaster scale the diverting and reassuring model of an ideal walk), just like Rimbaud's or Eberhardt's flight (she, by deciding never to return, is right in line with Rousseau and Thoreau in their obsession with walking), dates from a time when traveling took one to new places, with all the dangers that that implied. This was the era Hugo Pratt chose for his comic strip character, Corto Maltese, the perfect incarnation of the old-time traveler — Corto Maltese, the sailor with the springy step, the vagabond of the southern seas, the investigator of lagoons and hidden coves, the cynical adventurer, the elusive dreamer, the man whose only answer to the question, "Where are you going?" is: "Far. . ."

In those days, a voyage was not seen as one option for the holidays, a pause in work and profit-making. It was seen as part of the "business of living" and intelligence about life. It was not related to just one season, summer, but to a stage in a lifetime: youth. It met an internal need. This was in the 19th century, before the advent of tourism as an industry, before its seemingly peaceful imperialism (or murderous, actually, since it negates in one gesture both the traveler and the native, the visitor and his host, since, nullifying any meeting, it substitutes the known for the event of setting foot on foreign ground, substitutes the already-familiar or already figured-out for the avid eye of the traveler who is eager to see something new). The triumph of tourism, one of the dominant phenomena of the 20th century, is that it has mercilessly served everything up on a platter. Meticulously carving up the territory to be explored into chunks that match the timeframe available to the tourist, this sometimes leads to insane proposals — for example, how to see Venice in just one day.

Tourism is the fulfillment, the realization of a universe of desperation. This well-tempered hell engulfs every aspect of life, placing it all on stage, or running it through its reality-machine, turning into "authentic" experiences impressions from every part of the world, every activity, every gesture: the fabric dyers of Marrakech, the secondhand booksellers along the quays of the Seine, the reed weavers on Lake Titicaca, and the Hindus who light bonfires to burn their dead on the banks of the Ganges, in Benares. Nobody is safe. And anyone who thinks he has managed to keep himself out of the traveling mass of tourists has only become one of the petrified memories that they take back home with them. Thus, while I sit peacefully in Nice, eating a *socca*, on the cours Saleya, a group of Japanese tourists stops to photograph me — it's hilarious. Shall I come out with some memorable Niçoise phrases, toss my brunette curls and regale them with a song?

Guido Ceronetti, in *Un voyage en Italie*, takes on a rescue mission on behalf of his country and the very idea of travel. He tries to extract from the jumble of ugliness that he encounters some rare elements of still intact beauty. Upon his arrival in Sicily, he notes,

> But in Taormina one can only lose hope. There, the malignant spell of tourism removes all rela-

tionship to reality: in *tourism*, neither life nor death exists, neither happiness nor sorrow. There is only tourism, which is not the presence of something, but the removal of everything, in exchange for payment. The tourists are shadows and so are the tradesmen, the hotel keepers, the tour organizations, everything that is eaten or drunk, the mass held in the little church. . . . The hell of tourism is one of the worst, because you feel buried, locked up in stupidity like being trapped in a pyramid, and you are afraid they will forget you down there, that nobody will come to let you out. And Taormina is closed, it is hard to get into — which worsens the panic. Will I ever be able to leave? Will I pass the days, years, centuries, stepping out of my hotel to buy *The Times, Die Welt, The Guardian*, stamps and postcards, to eat an ice cream, to gaze in the shop windows at snowshoes and hiking boots, to send flowers home, to write to my stupid friends — "best wishes from this paradise"?

'We have swordfish today!'

'That's nice!'

'It's sunny today. *Sonne!*'

'Oh!'[13]

Ceronetti follows a course that alternates be-

13. Guido Ceronetti, *Un voyage en Italie*, translated from Italian into French by Andre Maugé, Paris, Albin Michel, 1996, p. 183-184.

tween bouts of rage (long) and enchantment (short).
It is marvelous because it has no value outside of itself. Labyrinthine, poetic, dreamy, contemplative,
with innumerable sidetracks and reversals, pauses at
the most unexpected, most forsaken places, at the
edge of cities and active life, away from the economic
circuits, the famous tourist attractions, in those
places where something stops, disjointed. The author
has a predilection for old people's homes, insane asy-
lums and abandoned villages, where nothing lives
anymore but the cobwebs, overgrown shrubbery, and
wild flowers. Visiting an asylum at Lucca, Ceronetti
comes up with a beautiful phrase, in connection with
the internees who are all sedated: they are "orphaned
from their madness". The expression does not apply
only to the residents of the institution, it applies to
all of us. And if his book is a guide, it is in the spiritual sense of rehabilitating, or reinhabiting the madness in ourselves, of recovering that side that has
been lost, that is slightly errant or simply not contemporary. If this voyage in the form of wandering
has any goal, it is to help us reach "the current of profound feelings", "the frisson of the infinite." This is
why Ceronetti uses such harsh words to berate two

plagues that hound us: thieves of time and thieves of silence. Together, they conspire to reduce us to the state of the "mental corpse".

Together, they are the backbone of organized tours: a continuous flow of highlights, without a pause, without a moment's lull, without the silent period that gives birth to a rhythm. Everything is gulped down at the same rate, with the same frigid voracity. We gorge ourselves on local cuisine, local music, local painting, Vivaldi, Guardi, Canaletto and cannellonis.

At the Ca'Rezzonico museum, the man standing next to me said, "Isn't it funny, the paintings show exactly what we see outside. There's no difference between the outdoors and indoors, nor between those days and now". And it's true, everything seems the same — except that we have been added to the picture. And, if you look closely enough, there are a few details, scenes, and gestures in the pictures that have disappeared since then. Here is a man standing thigh-deep in the water to push his gondola; you don't see that anymore; nor the young boys diving in the Grand Canal. That was a scene from the beginning of the 19th century, at a time when Byron was visiting Venice and could say, in all seriousness: "I like Venice as much as I expected to, and I expected much. . ." In Venice, he led a life of study and of vice. He swam, lounged on the beach of the Lido, and hosted parties. One night, in honor of a friend's departure, he hired Venetian singers who sang *The Death of Clorinde* while slowly gliding away from the Piazzetta, as in the days of yore. . .

Tourism provides an intensive effort at cultural re-animation — in vain. There is no sign of breathing. Almost no pulse. Was the heartbeat any stronger months ago when, in the subway, between two clumps of homeless men, the future traveler looked up from his newspaper and saw a brightly colored and competitive ad displayed on the station wall? Maybe. . . Amid all that chaos, it offered him (with great sloganeering about freedom) the lures of Malta, Malaga, Hammamet, Turkey, Sicily, Mauritius, Guadeloupe, Majorca, Tel-Aviv, Ghana, Greece ("Elected vacation paradise by His Majesty the Sun"), Egypt. . . He was seduced. He was aware of feeling worn down, fatigued. He dreamed that, over there, he would start to really look at things again, and change his ways; the way he did when he first moved to

Paris. But who knows? Maybe he really did open his eyes again, and maybe he was reinvigorated, and maybe this even extended, on his return, to the way he was living in his own city. Maybe.

Even without being locked into an organized tour, you feel the same asphyxiation, the same inability to form your own impressions of a place, to see and to sense the surroundings, when a well-intentioned person offers to serve as your local guide and then never leaves you alone. Thanks to him, you won't get lost and you won't miss seeing something "important". Your visit goes as smoothly as possible and you will only be able to speak positively about it (when you get back and people ask, "how did it go?" you can say, "it was great"). But you will have that insidious, annoying sense that *nothing happened*. Because this was the other person's place and the visit that he imposed on you had nothing to do with you, *per se*, nor him either. It was a refined, homogenized tour served up for transitory visitors, some kind of middle ground between his intimate experience and an introduction to some alien curiosity. In other words, it wasn't anybody's tour.

Once, to get out from under one such well-meaning guide, I invented a fictitious friend that I had to visit. I thus procured some free time for myself, without his overbearing tutelage. I enjoyed my free time so much that my "friend" had to become more and more demanding, in crisis. I invented a whole identity for her, a history. By the end of my stay, I hardly left this "friend" alone, so that when I would meet with my guide I had to discuss with him all of Lola's problems. (This fictitious friend, made up in order to preserve our solitude, is the inverse of those, more common, real friends whose existence we keep to ourselves!). This sense of being absent from oneself is felt even more strongly when we allow ourselves to be taken on a trip and we leave all the details of planning up to another person, allowing them to show us a country.

Colette tells us this story. One afternoon she received a visit from a young woman who said to her, pointing a finger at her nickel-plated car outside:

> 'I'll pick you up tomorrow morning! Be ready at
> seven and leave things for me. We'll lunch at B. . .
> at midday on the dot. We'll have a snack at C. . . at

four. And may my tongue be covered with ulcers if half past seven doesn't find us at D. . . , elbows on the table, with an aperitif.[14]

Colette declines the invitation. "You are, I repeat, perfect: I shan't travel with you." She prefers to have a little space, a little leeway. She savors the woods, the brooks, the lavender digitalis, the scent of the pines. . .

All this is mine, together with the rural silence, varied and accessible, that you can't hear; for nothing halts you on the road as you plunge through the smoke of the bakehouse fire and transfix the butterflies' flight.[15]

"The world is following you," said one of the first portable telephone advertisements; "Stay in touch with the ground while you are in the air", said another one, for Jet-phone. These are well-aimed shots, since people, for their part, stick to the world, to their world, and cannot tear themselves away. They never let go of the telephonic umbilical cord, visible or otherwise.

14. Colette, *Journey for Myself*, translated from French by David Le Vay. The Bobbs-Merrill Company, Indianapolis/New York: 1972; p. 44.
15. *Ibid*, p. 46.

The worst telephone calls come just before din-
ner, as a nauseated Guido Ceronetti notes:

> We get a good idea of what nonsense, what mis-
> ery we live in, on Saturday evenings. Just look at
> the phone booths with their doors darkened by
> people who are spitting words into the receivers,
> flailing around like vertical epileptics, biting at the
> telephone with alarming teeth, and digesting —
> like cannibals — the telephone, *the others* who are
> speaking to them from far away, making sure they
> still own them, enjoying their power over them
> (little children, and women especially!) — verita-
> ble man-eaters — stupid words, insignificant
> news, and clumsy arguments; and when the callers
> finally emerge, they actually seem to wipe their
> mouth as if they had just had a 'big meal', as if they
> were just finishing a prolonged coitus, their
> mouths still laughing at the idiocies they have
> swallowed. . .[16]

I'm watching a tourist at Torcello, sitting at the
edge of a tiny vineyard. He has eaten first, but that
was not enough. He comes out of the restaurant.
With one hand he telephones his mother, and with

---

16. Guido Ceronetti, *Un voyage en Italie, op. cit.*, p. 67-68.

the other hand he's about to take a picture of his wife and children. "I'm on a little island, I'm leaving a restaurant, I'm about to get on a big boat," he shouts. "Yes, Mom, it's beautiful, it's very beautiful." Shouting makes him angry. Suddenly he's furious. And since his mother over there is not responding, he shakes the telephone, then hands it to his wife: "You talk to her." His mother's silence is unbearable for him. He repeats: "Say hello. Say something to her. What's the matter, is she upset or something?" But the wife, posing to have her picture taken, doesn't move.

Neither traveler, nor tourist: the adventurer

Behind her, you can just make out the entrance to the Locanda Cipriani. I never go past that without thinking of a gondolier who told me he had once had Hemingway as a passenger: "He was drunk and happy. I was taking him home one night. He had been drinking at Harry's Bar. But he wanted to go on with me. Under the arbor. . ."

"I thought Hemingway only came to Venice in the winter, or in autumn to hunt ducks, and that he stayed at the Hotel Gritti."

"That's right. It was a look-alike. It was some guy who didn't let that kind of considerations stop him."

Hemingway was somebody who could to fall asleep, dead drunk, in the back of a gondola, but he was never too far gone to contemplate the stars. It was even the beauty of the heavens, the clearness of the night sky, that guided his choice of the countries in which he lived: Spain, Italy, Cuba. . . And it is the way the American novelists like Hemingway and Henry Miller lived, as much as the freshness, energy, and the extraordinary youth of their prose, that struck me when I discovered them. I was impressed by their easy way of traversing Europe, without haste, like strollers, free to go on or to stop as they wished.

"It is quite simply *there* that I should like to live", Roland Barthes wrote as a caption to Charles Clifford's photograph, *The Alhambra (Granada), 1854-1856*.[17] Those others, they actually did it. They found the owner of the house and persuaded him to rent it to

---

17. Roland Barthes, *Camera Lucida*, translated by Richard Howard. Flamingo, London: 1984; p. 38.

them for an unspecified period of time. They began a new life, in Paris, in Provence, in Venice, Madrid, Japan. . . They fell in love, learned a new language, discovered flavors and aromas, got caught up in the theater of the daily life that unfurled before them — with thousands of nuances and variations — the latest of their chosen places. *A Moveable Feast* is, in my eyes, the ultimate apprenticeship novel, a quick and indelible training, a new departure — a narrative that does not teach us to give a positive meaning to a setback, to turn pain into wisdom, but that waves them away with a flourish of the hand and sticks to questions of speed and balance, of decision-time, of relevance. It's a way of approaching the page, of never being in the wrong neighborhood or the wrong café. The title says it all. Hemingway's jubilation surged forth and became systematic in Paris, but it is mobile. It moves with him, to the Alps, for example, where Hemingway thought of "transplanting" himself when the bad season arrived.

> As I ate my oysters, with their strong taste of the sea, and their faint metallic taste that the cold white wine washed away, leaving only the sea taste and the succulent texture on the tongue, and

as I drank their cold liquid from each shell and washed it down with the crisp taste of the wine, I lost the empty feeling and began to be happy and to make plans."[18]

Hemingway shows us an art of letting go and getting intoxicated. It is not the wealth of descriptions that thrill us in reading Hemingway. I don't read him in order to be transported elsewhere, or to be hypnotized with exoticism, but so that, with his example, I can flee a world governed by models of efficiency, supported by the inertia of automatic responses. I don't read him in order to dream, in order to substitute new, more colorful, more sparkling images for those that surround me. I read him again and again in order to absorb his flexibility, to formulate another concept of life, nomadic, unencumbered, regulated by alternations of excitation and boredom, and one in which I can decide how long to stay in one place on the basis of some internal, hypersensitive and unpredictable clock. Hemingway's literature, like Henry Miller's, proposes a life shaped by impulses, animated and disturbed by fleeting, changing, contradictory impetuses; a chaotic life, but without

18. Ernest Hemingway, *A Moveable Feast*, Touchstone Books, Simon & Schuster, New York: 1996, p. 6.

the pangs of rending choices, the tragedy of the irreversible. It is an art of displacement, the knack of
seizing "the right moment to leave".

Long before the "lost generation" of the 20th century American writers, the grand master in this art
was Casanova. What we get from the exteriority that
is introduced by a foreign point of view — the perception of Europe without borders or barriers — we
get from Casanova's 18th century travels: the same
ease in moving from one city to another, from one
kingdom to another, Italy to France, Paris to St. Petersburg, Rome to Constantinople. This facility is
not due to the means of transportation and communication (slow, inconvenient, exhausting), but to the
lightness of not being tied to any place of origin. I
don't mean that it fades from memory or is denied —
Casanova never stops seeing himself as a Venetian —
but the refusal to acknowledge that it has any force of
law, any right of assignment. Venice, for a high flyer
like Casanova, implies preferences and complicities.
It is the optimal place to return to, because it does
not close in on the traveler, does not bind him with
the stability of a final engagement. Casanova always
returns to Venice, because it is the city-as-theater.

> I set out toward the Piazza San Marco, very curi-
> ous to see and to be seen by all my acquaintances,
> who could not be surprised to see me no longer
> dressed as an abate.[19]

He is burning to find out how the show is going, to
don his carnival mask again, to try out a new disguise.
As in the *commedia dell'arte*, the text is free and any im-
provisation is allowed. The intrigue includes interruptions. People are always leaving Venice — according to one constant: "I left with joy in my heart,
without regretting anything." This joy is at its height
when the departure is really an escape. After lan-
guishing for several months in the Piombi prisons,
Casanova flees, at dawn. He gets back into a gondola
and takes up his adventures where he had left off.

> I then turned and looked down the splendid
> canal; and seeing not a single boat and admiring
> the most beautiful day one could hope for.[20]

The fugitive is so happy that he bursts out sobbing
with tears of joy. And the descriptive narrative, awk-
ward, broken, disjointed from the fluidity of its sub-

---

19. Casanova Giacomo, *History of my life*, first translated into English in
accordance with the original French manuscript, by Willard R. Trask.
Harcourt, New York: 1966-70; Vol. 2, p.53.
20. *Ibid*, Vol. 4, p. 317.

ject, stops there. Casanova is wearing the only clothes that he has, the carnival dress that he was wearing when he was arrested. Here, at the break of day, the festival that he is celebrating with his tears is that of his own freedom.

History of My Life, as has often been said, makes for dull reading if we keep our distance and expect precise descriptions. Fellini compared it to reading a telephone directory. But if we regard these memoirs not as a window on a universe that has since disappeared, not as a nostalgic vision of scenes from the past, but as the narration of a life lived under the sign of the journey, then this work is an exciting blaze of passion — the passion of living one's life as though it were a play, of conceiving it as a work of art. Casanova entices us to organize (or disorganize) our present life to make it more intense, to flee with all our might everything that is wearisome, the mummifying power of habits, the anesthesia of the daily grind. Reading Casanova is an awakening, it reinvigorates the soul. It is the elixir of youth, which the charlatans of his day claimed to possess.

Casanova does not show us the sights of Rome or Venice as he knew them; he does better. He gives us the desire to tread the pavement with the same thirst for pleasure that drove him. He makes us disgusted for being satisfied with so little, for resigning ourselves to dull nights and morose mornings. "Fortune, Madam, is at work every day," he writes. And it is seducing Fortune that he incites us to practice! *Fortuna!* the goddess with the blindfold, the sightless dispenser of chance, it is She that he pursues; it is for Her, for the miraculous moment of her intervention, that he unfailingly adheres to his ethics of freedom, that he wants to make each day the ideal theater for her appearance. When he leaves a city, he does not go back to the places that he came from. Settling into his carriage, he considers his age and takes stock of his wealth and his physical condition. He evaluates his overall appeal. He constructs the scenario for his next stage. There are certain critical moments that he must work on particularly hard, like the moment of his arrival in the foreign city and the plot that he will construct around it, and other moments that he leaves to chance. For Fortune wants both, strategic precision and cold lucid analysis of the real state of our options, and a fuzzy enough backdrop to allow for the unforeseeable, the unthinkable, to occur. Fortune only comes (fleetingly, and with no promise as to tomorrow) to those who, monomaniacally dedicated to pleasure, understand nonetheless that satisfaction requires an art of distraction, floating, abandonment — a singular and paradoxical control within a lack of control. A kind of double game, a wandering eye that strays between unshakeable personal resolution and an acknowledgement that the world and circumstances hold unlimited power.

Casanova is a phenomenon of the will, but a will stripped of voluntarism and resting on a subtle and profound accord with that which is beyond him. Thus he can declare, in all serenity:

> I have loved women even to madness, but I have always preferred my freedom to them. When I have been in danger of sacrificing it, only chance has saved me.[21]

Don Giovanni acts according to a system, Casanova according to chance. He thinks of everything in terms of degrees of intensity, the heights of emotion and the upheavals that they represent. Even his desire to remain alone, to have multiple liaisons without being tied down, reflects his theatricality, his purism — his secret and constant concern with keeping himself available for Fortune, which follows only its

21. *Ibid*, vol. 3, p. 185.

own caprices and plays with people's destinies by rolling the dice. Casanova is not seeking new landscapes, but new situations. He is not a traveler but an adventurer: the brilliant director of his own life. In a rare moment Casanova is tempted, against his own rules, to leave Venice with a lover (the very beautiful M. M., locked up in the convent of Murano, and for whom chastity is a torment) and to share with her his wanderings; he ends up refusing.

> I should have had to leave Venice with her and I could not have returned there, and, her fate being linked with mine, my life would have been governed by a destiny entirely different."[22]

The design of his own life would have been messed up by hers, and along with the anguish of taking his chances, alone, the moment of his success would also disappear.

When I lived in Arizona (where the stars are so brilliant and seem so close that one night they frightened me) and I used to wonder whether I should move there permanently and continue to measure my fortune, luminous as it was, by the splendor of the

22. *Ibid.*, Vol. 4, p. 136.

mornings and the clarity of the air, or return to Paris (where happiness is measured differently!), I chose Paris over Tucson — because of the image that sometimes came to me, at around 6:00PM, the time for daydreaming around the swimming pool. I would see Paris at that time of day, at sundown, in a late-autumn fog, just as the lights are coming on. . . . Similarly, the same scene comes to me when I am on a journey, far from my red and gold volumes of *History of My Life*, and I think of Casanova: I always see him in his dressing gown in a spacious hotel room. His meal of twelve larks has been brought in, and a bottle of Bordeaux wine. He is getting ready for supper, with delicious anticipation, in front of a wood fire whose flames glitter in the diamonds of his rings. On the carpet sits an open trunk. Papers, books, piled up or one by one, lie at his feet; opened folders stand like fragile roofs, creating the same sort of inspired disorder that surrounds Saint Jerome in Carpaccio's painting. A superb dress is spread out on the bed, half hidden by the curtains. Gems shine in its folds. Casanova, with his quick dark eyes, glances that way. From one second to the next, the door might open, a woman might appear. Casanova is waiting without waiting. He is completely satisfied, in any event.

A QUESTION OF STYLE

Casanova made it a rule never to be bored, not to endure situations but always to vary them, subvert them, make them serve his pleasure. However, when he grew old, he had to depart from the exceptional mold to which the adventurer lays claim, by right, and join the common fold. Under the double constraint imposed by his lack of money and his decline of vigor, he accepted the hospitality of the Count von Waldstein, in Bohemia.

From then on, he led a sedentary existence, interrupted only by a few trips to Prague and visits to his friend the Prince of Ligne. He found the monotony depressing. He was distressed to be reduced to reading the newspapers in order to come across anything new. But, always insatiable, he very soon discovered a way to liven up the long years of retirement: by writing his memoirs and thereby refreshing the emotions of the first time; by celebrating the spirit of freedom until the end. Casanova, the performer, thus won on every score. After having conceived his life as a play or as a series of magic tricks, he then made it into a masterpiece. He bet everything on the moment. On a system of improvidence, he built a monument that has withstood the centuries. This endeavor took up all his energy. The days went by in a flash; his present was under the spell of the past, but was extended by the effort of recollecting, by projecting himself through his writing, and this gave him an enigmatic strength. The old man went on having fun. In spite of his complaints and his rages, Casanova is firmly on the side of those who, like Mme. du Barry, are prepared to plead with the Executioner, trying to get a few more minutes.

From his first steps as a child in Venice to the gates of death in that northern château, Casanova acquired considerable experience in the matter of happiness — but no philosophy of detachment. Predatory and violent, passionately hedonistic, without one ounce of cool, Casanova contradicted the wisdom of the Stoics and of Epictetus, who gave us an instructive allegory: "During a crossing, when the boat makes a stopover, you can disembark if you like, to get some water; you can pick up a shell, or an onion, but you must keep your attention fixed on the boat, you must keep turning back to look at it, in case the pilot is calling you. And if he calls you, then you must drop everything, if you do not want to be tied up and thrown into the hold, the way they do with the sheep. It is the same in life: maybe you will find yourself with a wife or a child, instead of an onion or a shell; nothing stands in the way of that. But if the pilot calls you, run to the boat, leave everything behind, don't look back. And if you are old, don't even allow yourself to get very far from the boat, or you might miss the call."

Casanova's greatest desire was, on the contrary, to miss that call, or, given the great number of passengers, to have the pilot embark someone else in his place.

The task of the pilot is certainly delicate, and it is astonishing that mistakes are not made, for he has to take into account not only the immense majority of refractory passengers who have to be strapped down to keep them from running and who, old and sick as they may be, still find ways to slip their bonds, but he also has to keep an eye on the minority, the tortuous, stubborn, unpredictable ones, those who are suicidal, those who have only one idea in their heads, to anticipate the call, to go when they choose to. They arrive, desperate, crushed, but despite everything, possessed of a strange air of triumph.

"Nobody was ever short of good reasons for killing himself," Pavese observed, referring to that humorous tone that is characteristic of people who are familiar with the idea of suicide — sometimes terrifying, sometimes comfortable, an inevitable and welcome partner, a matter of fate while being, at the same time, somewhat random. This idea surfaces in various forms and, within the range of black humor, can cause all sorts of moods from the most morbid to the most amusing. It can become an obsessive injunction that takes one prisoner, or a treasured last resort, inalienable, that delivers us from our destiny and makes us the master of our fate — just the way, in a love affair, it is the overt prospect of being able to bring it to an end at any time that keeps it alive, in the same way, at the heart of one's relationship with oneself, there is always this alternative, the choice of going on or stopping.

"Where does this vague, profound, *fundamental* joy come from, that wells up in the veins and throat of those who have decided to commit suicide? In the face of death, nothing remains anymore but the brutal awareness of still being alive," Pavese wrote in his journal, in February 1938. Later published as *Il mestiere di vivere* [published in English as *The Burning Brand*, and as *This Business of Living*], the journal is an ardent meditation on the relationship between the "trade" of living — a slow, arduous apprenticeship, learned and tested with the passing of the years — and the single gesture of committing suicide. It is a subtle relationship, since being able to seize, in a timely way, the difficult moment of taking your leave would be proof that you have actually mastered the trade and may even have a special knack for it. The idea of suicide ends up being obvious when, as a consequence of weariness and the exhaustion of your "vital stock", you can no longer have any active and positive role in "protesting life". And it is inescapable when, in the face of death, you no longer feel the overwhelming sensation of still being alive, when you no longer feel anything anymore.

But then, isn't it too late to still find the energy to commit suicide? And therein lies the suspense. The line that separates life from death may be fragile, albeit irreversible, but the line that separates life from the non-life that is its ghost-like or mechanical perpetuation, lacking any sense of belonging to oneself, lacking any well-reflected plan, any mental or physical desire, is at least as thin. And it is this death before death that was first used to assassinate the deportees of Auschwitz. In *If This is a Man*, Primo Levi writes that he had nothing left of his life from those days but the strength to endure the hunger and the cold, adding that he was not alive enough anymore to be capable of doing himself in. He finally committed suicide in 1987, in Turin, his birthplace.

"How dead you have to be, that you don't even want to die anymore," Pavese noted on January 1, 1950. It seemed to him that it was already too late, that he had sunk into a way of life that was tanta-

mount to having already committed suicide; but, in
summer of the same year, on August 27, he found that
wish still intact, and fulfilled it. By this gesture, he
saved his life. He gave it form and significance and, as
he had done for his books, imprinting it with his own
style.

You have spent the day in cafés, trying to
quench a thirst that nothing seems to alleviate. And
now, without hesitating, deciphering the extinguished letters on its neon sign, you enter the first
hotel you come to. You ask for a room. They tell you
that 34 is free, do you want to look at it? No need.
They hand you the key, with an absentminded smile,
while outside the swallows are whirling and the
chime of vespers wafts in from the church nearby.
Your room is on the third floor. You have no trouble
finding it. You open the window, breathe in the hot
air — the air of a town, with the scent of hay. You
look out at the roofs, the hills. You look for the
river — there it is, so near. It sparkles through your
tears and you do not know how to drink in enough of

this landscape of woods and orchards. But the tears stop as abruptly as they started, and you turn your back to the window. The room is white, clean and spartan. You notice, by reflex, that there is no reading light. It is a room like any other. A room you are just passing through.

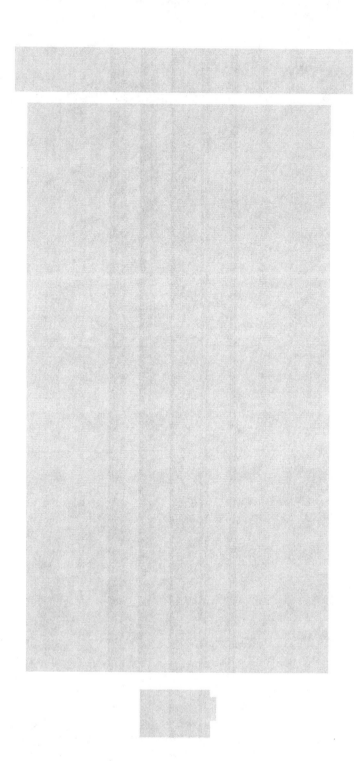

Also from Algora Publishing:

CLAUDIU A. SECARA
THE NEW COMMONWEALTH:
FROM BUREAUCRATIC CORPORATISM TO SOCIALIST CAPITALISM

The notion of an elite-driven worldwide perestroika has gained some credibility lately. The book examines in a historical perspective the most intriguing dialectic in the Soviet Union's "collapse" — from socialism to capitalism and back to socialist capitalism — and speculates on the global implications.

DOMINIQUE FERNANDEZ
PHOTOGRAPHER: FERRANTE FERRANTI
ROMANIAN RHAPSODY — An Overlooked Corner of Europe

"Romania doesn't get very good press." And so, renowned French travel writer Dominique Fernandez and top photographer Ferrante Ferranti head out to form their own images. In four long journeys over a 6-year span, they uncover a tantalizing blend of German efficiency and Latin nonchalance, French literature and Gypsy music, Western rationalism and Oriental mysteries. Fernandez reveals the rich Romanian essence. Attentive and precise, he digs beneath the somber heritage of communism to reach the deep roots of a European country that is so little-known.

IGNACIO RAMONET
THE GEOPOLITICS OF CHAOS

The author, Director of Le Monde Diplomatique, presents an original, discriminating and lucid political matrix for understanding what he calls the "current disorder of the world" in terms of Internationalization, Cyberculture and Political Chaos.

TZVETAN TODOROV
A PASSION FOR DEMOCRACY – BENJAMIN CONSTANT

The French Revolution rang the death knell not only for a form of society, but also for a way of feeling and of living; and it is still not clear what we have gained from the changes. Todorov examines the life of Constant, one of the original thinkers who conceptualized modern democracy, and in the process gives us a richly textured portrait of a man who was fully engaged in life, both public and private.

MICHEL PINÇON & MONIQUE PINÇON-CHARLOT
GRAND FORTUNES – DYNASTIES OF WEALTH IN FRANCE

Going back for generations, the fortunes of great families consist of far more than money—they are also symbols of culture and social interaction. In a nation known for democracy and meritocracy, piercing the secrets of the grand fortunes verges on a crime of lèse-majesté . . . Grand Fortunes succeeds at that.

CLAUDIU A. SECARA
TIME & EGO – Judeo-Christian Egotheism and the Anglo-Saxon Industrial Revolution

The first question of abstract reflection that arouses controversy is the problem of Becoming. Being persists, beings constantly change; they are born and they pass away. How can Being change and yet be eternal? The quest for the logical and experimental answer has just taken off.

PASCAL BRUCKNER
THE TEMPTATION OF INNOCENCE – Living in the Age of Entitlement

"Gracefully erudite, deliciously mordant, Bruckner takes on a recent species of human self-deception: infantilism and victimization, the idea that powerlessness is a virtue without responsibility. This highly insightful essay dissects the culture of dependency and its damaging effects on the moral fiber of society, from corporate welfare to affirmative action.." *PublishersWeekly*
Académie française Prix 2000; Medici Prize for Essays

PHILIPPE TRÉTIACK
ARE YOU AGITÉ? Treatise on Everyday Agitation

The 'Agité,' that human species that lives in international airports, jumps into taxis while dialing the cell phone, eats while clearing the table, reads the paper while watching TV and works during vacation – has just been given a new title. "A book filled with the exuberance of a new millennium, full of humor and relevance. Philippe Trétiack, a leading reporter for Elle, takes us around the world and back at light speed." — Aujourd'hui le Parisien

PAUL LOMBARD
VICE & VIRTUE — Men of History, Great Crooks for the Greater Good

Personal passion has often guided powerful people more than the public interest. With what result? From the courtiers of Versailles to the back halls of Mitterand's government, from Danton — revealed to have been a paid agent for England — to the shady bankers of Mitterand's era, from the buddies of Mazarin to the builders of the Panama Canal, Paul Lombard unearths the secrets of the corridors of power. He reveals the vanity and the corruption, but also the grandeur and panache that characterize the great. This cavalcade over many centuries can be read as a subversive tract on how to lead.

RICHARD LABÉVIÈRE
DOLLARS FOR TERROR — The U.S. and Islam

"In this riveting, often shocking analysis, the U.S. is an accessory in the rise of Islam, because it manipulates and aids radical Moslem groups in its shortsighted pursuit of its economic interests, especially the energy resources of the Middle East and the oil- and mineral-rich former Soviet republics of Central Asia. Labévière shows how radical Islamic fundamentalism spreads its influence on two levels, above board, through investment firms, banks and shell companies, and clandestinely, though a network of drug dealing, weapons smuggling and money laundering. This important book sounds a wake-up call to U.S. policy-makers." — Publishers Weekly

JEANNINE VERDÈS-LEROUX
DECONSTRUCTING PIERRE BOURDIEU — *Against Sociological Terrorism
From the Left*

Sociologist Pierre Bourdieu went from widely-criticized to widely-acclaimed, without adjusting his hastily constructed theories. Verdès-Leroux suggests that Bourdieu arrogated for himself the role of "total intellectual" and proved that a good offense is the best defense. A pessimistic Leninist bolstered by a ponderous scientific construct, Bourdieu stands out as the ultimate doctrinaire more concerned with self-promotion than with democratic intellectual engagements.

HENRI TROYAT
TERRIBLE TZARINAS

Who should succeed Peter the Great? Upon the death of this visionary and despotic reformer, the great families plotted to come up with a successor who would surpass everyone else — or at least, offend none. But there were only women — Catherine I, Anna Ivanovna, Anna Leopoldovna, Elizabeth I. These autocrats imposed their violent and dissolute natures upon the empire, along with their loves, their feuds, their cruelties. Born in 1911 in Moscow, Troyat is a member of the Académie française, recipient of Prix Goncourt.

DEBORAH SCHURMAN-KAUFLIN
THE NEW PREDATOR: WOMEN WHO KILL —
Profiles of Female Serial Killers

This is the first book ever based on face-to-face interviews with women serial killers. Dr. Schurman-Kauflin analyzes the similarities and differences between male and female serial killers and mass murderers.

JEAN-MARIE ABGRALL
HEALING OR STEALING — *Medical Charlatans in the New Age*

Jean-Marie Abgrall is Europe's foremost expert on cults and forensic medicine. In his recent work, he examines the benefits and shortcomings of alternative medicines, helping the public to discern therapists from quacks. While not all systems of nontraditional medicine are linked to cults, he does suggest that many are futile if not downright harmful, and indeed can be used as an avenue of cult recruitment. The crisis of the modern world may be leading to a new mystique of medicine, where patients check their powers of judgment at the door.

RÉMI KAUFFER
DISINFORMATION — US Multinationals at War with Europe

"Spreading rumors to damage a competitor, using 'tourists' for industrial espionage. . . Kauffer shows how the economic war is waged." — Le Monde

"A specialist in the secret services, Kauffer notes that, 'In the CNN era, with our skies full of satellites and the Internet expanding every nano-second, the techniques of mass persuasion that were developed during the Cold War are still very much in use – only their field of application has changed.' His analysis is shocking, and well-documented." — La Tribune

CARL A. DAVIES
PLANE TRUTH — A PRIVATE INVESTIGATOR'S STORY

"Raises new questions about corporate and tribal loyalties, structural engineering, and money and politics, in a credible scenario that makes my flesh creep. . . I think I'll take a train, next time. Or walk." — Western Review

"Takes us around the world and finds treasure under stones that had been left unturned After reading these 'travels with Carl,' (or is he Sherlock Holmes?), my own life seems very flat." — Book Addicts

JENNIFER FURIO
LETTERS FROM PRISON — VOICES OF WOMEN MURDERERS

Written by incarcerated women, these incredibly personal, surprisingly honest letters shed light on their lives, their crimes and the mitigating circumstances. Author Jennifer Furio, a prison reform activist, subtly reveals the biases if the criminal justice system and the media. The words of these women haunt and transfix even the most skeptical reader.

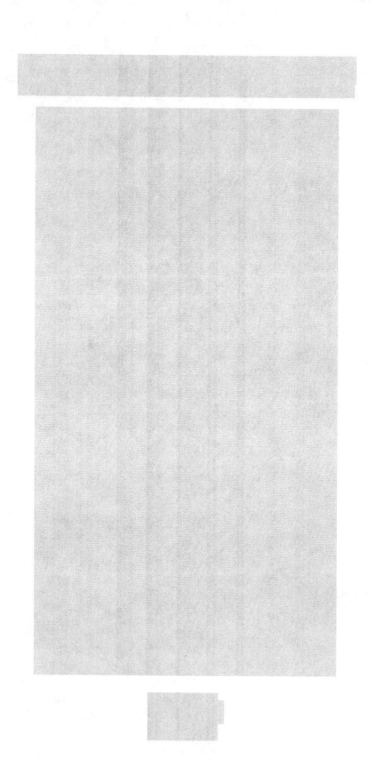